Book 1:
The Best of Spain for Tourists
BY GETAWAY GUIDES

&

Book 2:
The Best of Beautiful Greece for Tourists
BY GETAWAY GUIDES

&

Book 3:
The Best of Italy for Tourists

BY GETAWAY GUIDES

&

Book 4:
The Best of Beautiful Germany for Tourists
BY GETAWAY GUIDES

&

Book 5:
The Best of Beautiful France for Tourists
BY GETAWAY GUIDES

Book 1:
The Best of Spain for Tourists
BY GETAWAY GUIDES

The Ultimate Guide to Spain's Sites, Restaurants, Shopping, and Beaches for Tourists!

Travel Guide Box Set #20: The Best of Spain for Tourists + The Best of Beautiful Greece for Tourists + The Best of Italy for Tourists + The Best of Beautiful Germany for Tourists + The Best of Beautiful France for Tourists

Copyright 2014 by Getaway Guides - All rights reserved.

In no way is it legal to reproduce, duplicate, or transmit any part of this document in either electronic means or in printed format. Recording of this publication is strictly prohibited and any storage of this document is not allowed unless with written permission from the publisher. All rights reserved.

Travel Guide Box Set #20: The Best of Spain for Tourists + The Best of Beautiful Greece for Tourists + The Best of Italy for Tourists + The Best of Beautiful Germany for Tourists + The Best of Beautiful France for Tourists

Table Of Contents

Introduction 5

Chapter 1 - Restaurants 6

Chapter 2 - Beaches 8

Chapter 3 - Galleries and Museums 10

Chapter 4 - Shopping Districts 13

Chapter 5 - Natural Wonders 15

Chapter 6 - Amusement Parks 17

Conclusion 19

Travel Guide Box Set #20: The Best of Spain for Tourists + The Best of Beautiful Greece for Tourists + The Best of Italy for Tourists + The Best of Beautiful Germany for Tourists + The Best of Beautiful France for Tourists

Introduction

I want to thank you and congratulate you for purchasing the book, *"The Best of Spain for Tourists."*

This book contains proven steps and strategies on how to enjoy your vacation in one of the most beautiful countries in Europe. It will inform you about various tourist hot spots such as malls, amusement parks, beaches, museums, and a whole lot more.

This book is perfect for tourists who have never set foot in Spain before. But if you have been in the country numerous times, you should also peruse some of its pages because there might be other destinations that you have not yet visited.

Thanks again for purchasing this book, I hope you enjoy it!

Travel Guide Box Set #20: The Best of Spain for Tourists + The Best of Beautiful Greece for Tourists + The Best of Italy for Tourists + The Best of Beautiful Germany for Tourists + The Best of Beautiful France for Tourists

Chapter 1 – Restaurants

Spain is a country that is filled with a lot of delightful restaurants. Whether you are a lavish spender or a traveler with a tight budget, you can easily find an eatery that will suit your tastes and preferences. Aside from the menu, the designs of these establishments are all carefully planned to make sure that everyone will have a pleasant dining experience. Here is a list of their must-visit restaurants.

1. ABaC, Barcelona

This one is considered by most people as the rising star in the Spanish culinary scene. The owner, Jordi Cruz, got his first cooking experience at a restaurant called L'Estany Clar in Berga. At the young age of 26, he managed to snag the Michelin star award during his stint in this place. He is the youngest chef in the country to ever receive such a prestigious honor. With his skill and experience in the field of cooking, you can ensure that ABaC is one of the best restaurants in town.

Some of their best dishes include a smoked salmon with a rich cauliflower puree, and the mushroom and truffle focaccio. They also have a wide array of liquors to choose from. You can order their frothy champignon bisque, or the gin tonic that is made using cucumber and lemon sorbet.

2. Casa Bigote, Sanlúcar de Barrameda (Andalucía)

Sanlúcar de Barrameda is a town that is famous for their flavorful sherry, especially the Manzanilla variety. This type of spirit is best drunk while watching the sunset on a beach. And to make the experience better, you should definitely pair your Manzanilla with a plate of tapa from Casa Bigote. Their meals are very authentic and raffish. Dining in Casa Bigote is a memorable experience because the building provides a very light and casual atmosphere.

Since this restaurant started as a fisherman's tavern, its interior is well-decorated with various oddities that were caught in the fishermen's nets. It is also the reason why their menu consists of underwater delights such as prawns, shellfish, and fishes.

3. El Invernadero

If you grew tired and hungry after shopping in the upper markets in Salamanca, Madrid, then you can satiate your grumbling stomach by dining in El Invernardo. It is found near Serrano Street, where most of the designer stores are located. In order to complement its neighboring luxury shops, the exterior and interior of the restaurant looks and feels top notch. It has a well-lit terrace that is ideal for a romantic dinner date. The walls are also lined with glass pieces and modern paintings that greatly improved the insides of the restaurant.

Travel Guide Box Set #20: The Best of Spain for Tourists + The Best of Beautiful Greece for Tourists + The Best of Italy for Tourists + The Best of Beautiful Germany for Tourists + The Best of Beautiful France for Tourists

Their menu mostly consists of Mediterranean cuisine that is infused with Spanish cooking techniques. They serve Iberian ham and chorizos, vegetable salads, lamb chops, baby squid, and a bevy of other meals that are made from fish. For dessert, they have apple tarts, cakes, and ice creams.

4. La Vaca Argentina – Covarrubias

This eatery can be found on the Alonso Martinez section of central Madrid. True to its name, La Vaca Argentina prides itself in creating scrumptious, juicy, and mouth-watering meat dishes. They have bife de lomo, bife de chorizo, pecho de pollo, arrachera, and other types of meaty dishes. They also serve other meals such as pizza, pasta, empanadas, and ensaladas.

5. La Boquería Market: Bar Pinotxo and El Quim de la Boquería

La Boqueria is one of the best and biggest food markets in the world. And inside this market are two well-known bars – Pinotxo and Quinn. Although both of them are relatively small, they are very famous in La Boqueria because of their festive dishes. In Pinotxo, you should definitely try Chef Jordi Asin's meanmongetes amb sepia. This is made of little white beans and baby squids that are infused with balsamic vinegar. Another bestseller is the hisberberechos, or more commonly known as steamed cockles.

Over at El Quim, they have deep fried alcachofas, or artichoke hearts that are cooked with aioli. The owner, Quim Marquez Duran, can also whip up some other meals such as grilled clams, cava roast and green asparagus with rose cava.

6. Can Fabes

If you are searching for fine classic Spanish cuisine, you should head over to this restaurant. The management team at Can Fabes encourages their diners to stay, talk with friends and enjoy the evening for as long as they like. With their vast array of meat, vegetable and fish dishes, who would want to leave this place anyway? It is not that they do not have enough customers. They are always full, especially at night. They just love to give their customers the best time of their lives. This establishment is the first Catalan restaurant to ever receive the Michelin 3-star award.

7. Martin Berasategui

In order to create the boldest and richest flavors in their meals, this restaurant combines traditional cooking and scientific methods. In addition, their service is always exemplary, so you will rarely hear other people say negative things about them. Their most popular meals include grilled fish with chili and fish snout that is smoked to perfection.

Travel Guide Box Set #20: The Best of Spain for Tourists + The Best of Beautiful Greece for Tourists + The Best of Italy for Tourists + The Best of Beautiful Germany for Tourists + The Best of Beautiful France for Tourists

Chapter 2 - Beaches

With more than 5,000 miles of breathtaking and sandy coastline, searching for a beach in this country can be a very easy task. Tourists usually flock towards popular areas such as Costa Blanca, or Costa del Sol. However, there are still other beaches that are as beautiful as the two but less congested and more peaceful.

1. Illas Cies

This beach is more popularly called by the local people as the "Galician Caribbean." Illias Cies is composed of three sparkling and pristine neighboring islands that are found on Galicia – the northwest area of the country. One of their sides is slightly exposed to the Atlantic Ocean's mighty waves. However, their further sides are facing the aquatic haven that is known as Ria de Vigo. It is a calm and protected estuary that is teeming with exotic marine life.

The Illa de Monte Ayudo, along with its neighboring island the Illa do Faro, are both connected to the Rodas Beach. It is a pretty beach with cool, blue waters, and fine white sands. Illas Cies is slightly undeveloped because the authorities are preserving its natural beauty. Modern travelers do not need to worry about getting bored here because there are beach bars, campgrounds, markets and restaurants that are near the vicinity.

2. La Concha Beach - San Sebastian, Spain

Although beaches in isolated areas are dazzling and breathtaking, it does not mean that the ones near the cities are ugly. In fact, you can also find beauty and peace in some beaches that are near modern infrastructures. An example of this one is the La Concha Beach. This one offers a splendid view of its neighboring urban sprawl. It also helps that San Sebastian has a very mountainous topography.

La Concha's sandy curves measure 130 feet wide and 4,500 feet long. It encircles the Bay of La Concha, making it a tough contender for the title of world's most beautiful urban beaches. Since it offers a quick getaway from the city life, expect that a lot of yuppies and urban dwellers visit here on a regular basis. If you love to party and meet a lot of people, this beach is perfect for you.

3. Las Playas del Puerto de Santa María

The first thing that you need to know about this place is that it is very difficult to reach if you do not own or rent a car. There are no buses or any form of public transport that can take you there directly. However, this disadvantage can still be beneficial for people who are looking for a quiet place to swim and rest. Since there are only a few people, you can fully enjoy its other amenities such as restaurants, bars, heladarias, and a whole lot more. And when you are tired of swimming and basking in the sun, you can go on an adventure and visit the abandoned castle nearby.

4. Playa de Bolonia

The Andalusian region, which is in Tarifa, is a vast area where the country's biggest and highly popular beach destinations can be found. Some of them, including Marbella, are always teeming with a lot of tourists. However, there is still one beach in Andalusia that is not yet utterly unblemished. If you have the tenacity to trek Bolonia's fishing village, you will be able to reach Playa de Bolonia.

This beach has a shoreline which measures up to 2.4 miles. It curves around the Bolonia Bay as well as some rocky outcrops. This place is very peaceful and quiet, giving you ample space to relax or play in the sand. High winds regularly blow at Playa de Bolonia, making it one of the best windsurfing hubs in the country. But since only a handful of people visit here, expect that there are only basic amenities. If you want to go on a fun adventure, you can also visit the ancient ruins of Baelo Claudio which is just near the beach.

5. Zahara de las Atunes

It is located near the Costa de la Luz and the little fishing village called Zahara de las Atunes. This is one of the country's 648 beaches that were awarded with the "blue flag" title. The blue flag means that this is a natural tourist attraction that is extremely popular and pristine. Its sandy shores stretch up to 20 km.

6. Es Trenc, Balearic Islands

Although most beaches in the isles of Mallorca are already part of huge resorts, Es Trenc is still untouched by these enterprises. It is an isolated oasis that is replete with sand dunes and a thick forest of pines.

The light golden-colored and fine sand of this natural wonder greatly complement the crystal blue waves that lap gently on the shoreline. A lot of tourists who visited this hidden paradise said that the waters and sand can be greatly compared to a luxurious Caribbean beach. The Es Trenc beach is very shallow and tranquil which makes it an all-time favorite for families who have little children.

Travel Guide Box Set #20: The Best of Spain for Tourists + The Best of Beautiful Greece for Tourists + The Best of Italy for Tourists + The Best of Beautiful Germany for Tourists + The Best of Beautiful France for Tourists

Chapter 3 – Galleries and Museums

Galleries and museums are sanctuaries for people who are too tired with the hustle and bustle of the city. They may not be as serene as a beach, but these establishments are still good places to visit if you want to loosen up a bit. In addition, it is also nice to learn a little bit of history every once in a while. You will be amazed at how old paintings and ancient artifacts can amaze you. If you are planning to visit Spain, you should definitely check out these galleries and museums.

1. Museo Thyssen-Bornemisza

This museum in Madrid actually played a big role in European art revolution. The 700 canvasses that were included in this collection were all acquired by a European art collector back in 1920. The masterpieces were officially put on view in Lugano, Switzerland before Madrid managed to acquire it in the 1980s. This museum boasts of 700 canvasses and works from various artists such as El Greco and Picasso. In fact, one can say that it greatly rivaled the personal collection of the Royal Queen. Each masterpiece was meticulously arranged in chronological order, making it easier for the tourists to see how European art evolved through the ages.

2. Museo de Arte Abstracto Español

The beauty of this museum in Cuenca lies in the establishment's angular medieval design. It effectively complemented its stellar collection of modern masterpieces. Back in the 1950s and 1960s, a lot of popular Spanish artists settled here in Cuence. Some of them include Antoni Tapes, Luis Feito, and Fernando Zobel. If you are a fan of these masters, you will definitely be glad to hear that a lot of their creations are displayed in Museo de Arte.

3. Museo Nacional de Escultura, Valladolid

The masterpieces that were part of Museo Nacional de Escultura's collection are great proofs of the wonderful achievements that the Spanish artists have accomplished during the Middle Ages up to the 19th century. Each artwork weaves a tale of interaction with foreign lands, evolution of artistic influences, and other vital contexts about the European culture before.

The very first pieces that were included in the collection were acquired from the various covenants that were disentailed across Valladolid and some of its neighboring areas. Each artwork that you will see in this collection was well preserved by the people. This shows how the city is passionate about conserving the beauty of each masterpiece.

Aside from paintings, you will also see various sculptures in this museum. The beauty of these artworks greatly represents the country's love for everything that is beautiful and artistic.

4, Museo-Hospital de Santa Cruz

This art gallery in Toledo was first developed by the town's archbishop as a hospital that caters to the impoverished masses. This museum was popular among the art enthusiasts because of its very Plateresque architecture. It has a very intricate façade that makes the interior more beautiful rather than complex or intimidating. However, the real treasure of this museum lies in its collection. It had several artworks that were traced back from the 16th to the 17th century. They also have the 18 masterpieces that were created by the great El Greco himself. This includes his stellar masterpiece called the Altar of the Assumption, which was finished back in 1613 before his untimely death. Moreover, the museum also holds a bevy of more primitive paintings.

5. Museo de Arte Moderno, Tarragona

This vast museum was developed by the deputy of Tarragona back in 1976. This is to ensure that the artistic patrimony of the area will be greatly preserved and remembered. The collections found in Museo de Arte Morderno were acquired back in the sixties. The very first masterpieces that were acquired were Julio Antonio's sculpted creations. After that, more collections were purchased thanks to the help of Lluis M. Saumells, Tarragona's School of Arts director. Other vital pieces that can be found in the museum are the sculptures that were developed by Santiago Costa I Vaque, and Salvador Martorelli I Olle.

6. The Museum of Art Noveau and Art Deco

This one is one of the youngest museums in Spain. Although it just recently opened in April 1995, it was one of the most popular art galleries in the Castile and Leon areas. In fact, it is estimated that more than 120,000 people visit this museum a year.

Over the last decade, these museums, as well as its sponsor Manuel Ramos Andrade, have amassed various recognitions for their contributions and efforts in improving the culture and tourism in the region. Some of these include the City Gold Medal, Master de Poularidad, and the Paul Harris Fellowship award.

This museum was so popular that His Highness Felipe de Borbón y Grecia came here in 1997 to visit the place. In addition, Queen Sofia and several of the First Ladies of various countries also privately visited the establishment back in 2005.

These royalties were enthralled by the Andrade Foundation's vast collection of dolls, jewels, and scented bottles.

7. Museo Nacional de Arte Romano, Mérida

This one specializes in collecting ancient Roman sculptures that were found in Merida. They managed to unearth various relics such as tombs, amphitheaters, mini-theaters and several artistic objects. In order to complement the collection, the architect of the museum borrowed some Roman design theories to make the place look fabulous.

Travel Guide Box Set #20: The Best of Spain for Tourists + The Best of Beautiful Greece for Tourists + The Best of Italy for Tourists + The Best of Beautiful Germany for Tourists + The Best of Beautiful France for Tourists

Chapter 4 – Shopping Districts

Their shopping districts may not be as vast as the ones that are found in London, but their collection of shops and fashion boutiques is still vast enough to satisfy your shopping needs. Below is a list of Spain's best and busiest shopping districts.

1. Ramblas and Old Town

The alleyways of Barcelona are always filled with small shops. Most of them have survived tough competitions from other bigger stores because the community still patronizes them. These small stores may not sell luxury brands, but they still offer goods that are lovely and fine. In these places, you can find sweets, souvenirs, tasty wine and snacks.

The Placa Catalunya in the upper side of Ramblas, Barcelona is one of the biggest department stores in the area. Near the vicinity is another shopping temple called El Corte Ingles.

If you are looking for food, La Boqueria is the best place to go. It is a modernist market that offers fresh fruits, vegetables, meat and fish.

2. Xanadu Commercial and Leisure Center

This is located in Madrid and is known as one of the biggest shopping districts in the city. It has more than 250 stalls that are open every day. Aside from the stalls, the district also has cinema houses and restaurants that you can explore after you are finished buying your clothes. If you are searching for other forms of entertainment, you can also try Xanadu's go-kart racing course, amusement park, and the bowling alley.

The establishment also has its very own indoor ski slope. The slopes for beginners and experts are separated.

3. Príncipe Pío Shopping Center

This place has already been a busy shopping district ever since it was established in the 19th century. There was once a very old railroad in the vicinity, but now it was turned into a huge shopping mall. However, they still managed to maintain the original structure of the place. These days, Principe Pio is lined with stores, cinema houses and restaurants.

4. Dreams Palacio de Hielo

Aside from the expansive shopping mall, Palacio de Hielo prides itself in having a splendid ice skating rink that measures more than 1,800 square meters. There are also other amenities that you can try here such as an indoor swimming pool, gym, bowling area and a solarium.

5. Gran Via & Sol

If you are looking for a shopping center that sells luxurious brands, then this is the place where you should go. In this region, retail fashion stores such as Amancio Gaona's Inditex dominate the scene. In here, you can see all your favorite brands such as Zara, Stradivarius, Top Man, Marks & Spencer, Guess, and a whole lot more.

6. El Corte Inglés

El Corte Inglés is an omnipresent department store chain that is scattered around the country. It is very convenient because you can buy all of the things that you want here. Not only do they sell luxury brands, they also offer products that the masses can buy.

Travel Guide Box Set #20: The Best of Spain for Tourists + The Best of Beautiful Greece for Tourists + The Best of Italy for Tourists + The Best of Beautiful Germany for Tourists + The Best of Beautiful France for Tourists

Chapter 5 – Natural Wonders

Tired of the hustle and bustle in the city? Why not visit Spain's natural wonders? These places may not have extremely fancy restaurants, wild clubs and Wi-Fi hot spots, but are still magnificent and beautiful.

1. Picos de Europa

The biggest attraction that Picos de Europa has to offer is its extremely long and high cable car. From Fuente De, this machine can transport you up to 1850 meters above the rock faces in under four minutes. It may sound a little bit dizzying, but the dazzling view of the alpine meadows is so breathtaking that you will definitely forget that you are nauseated. This cable car is one of the longest in the world.

If you have a great fear of heights, you can stay at the bottom of the cliffs and enjoy some of the other amenities in the place. There are campsites and a couple bars that offer great food and relaxation. And for thrill seekers, they can also hike around Peña Vieja or Pico Tesorero. However, be warned that the trip can be quite lengthy since the entire trip measures up to 2,570 meters.

2. The magnificent waters of Cabo de Gata

In Cabo de Gata, one of the best beaches that you can visit is Playo de Monsul. It is surrounded by large volcanic rocks that were intricately sculptured by nature. The entrance of this place is a barchans sand dune. The beach structure is an effect of fossil volcanism that happened before across the Iberian Peninsula. This occurred when the plates of Eurasia and Africa collided together during the ancient times.

3. Castellfollit de la Roca

This small town in Catalonia only has 1,000 inhabitants, which make it an ideal tourist destination for people who do not enjoy crowded areas. The place is situated on top of a basalt crag that is a kilometer in length and more than 50 meters in height. Thousands of years ago, volcanic eruptions are frequent in this place. And after some time, the rivers Fluvia and Toronell washed away the debris from these volcanic eruptions. Although the town is approximately just a square kilometer in length, they are happy to welcome any tourists who are willing to drop by and marvel at the beauty of the place.

4. La Gomera

This is part of the country's Canary Islands which is found near the Atlantic Ocean and African coast. This is considered as the second smallest piece of land among the 6 other regions that are also part of the Canary Islands. This place is created due to volcanic eruptions. It is quite circular in shape and has a diameter of 22 kilometers. Its height, on the other hand, reaches up to 5000 feet. La Gomera's highest peak is the Garajonay.

5. Mallos de Riglos

This place has elegantly carved natural rock formations that are located in Huesca. Mallos de Riglos makes up some of the foothills of the Pyrenees. Almost all of the rocks that you will see here originated from the Miocene period.

Most climbers dream of climbing these rocky cliffs, which measure almost 300 meters in height. A lot of outdoor enthusiasts visit this natural wonder on a regular basis to challenge their skills, or just wander around and appreciate the rock's splendor.

There are several possible routes that you can take on this journey. However, some of the more demanding ones are quite harsh to the tender-footed adventurers. There are instances wherein you have to spend a night in a small tent that is attached to one of the rock faces.

If you are already a seasoned climber, you can find the challenge that you seek in El Puro, Castilla, Frenchin, and Visera cliffs.

6. Arribes del Duero

This travel hot spot offers a stunning view of the gorge that acts as a border between Spain and Portugal. It cuts along granite rocks and has a length of eighty kilometers. The cliffs, on the other hand, measure up to 200 meters. These high peaks are a haven for various types of birds such as golden eagles and griffon vultures. In order to get there, you can arrange a boat ride at Froteira de Zamora. During this trip, you will be able to see the massive hydroelectric dams that were constructed on the river.

Arribes de Duerro also has a natural park, which covers more than a hundred hectares of land. Beside it is another nature reserve that is built by the Portugese. When combined, these two areas make up one the biggest protected lands across Europe.

Travel Guide Box Set #20: The Best of Spain for Tourists + The Best of Beautiful Greece for Tourists + The Best of Italy for Tourists + The Best of Beautiful Germany for Tourists + The Best of Beautiful France for Tourists

Chapter 6 – Amusement Parks

Every large country has its very own theme parks. Whether you are a kid or an adult, you will definitely enjoy the roller coasters and other cool rides that are found in Spain.

1. Terra Mitica, Benidorm

True to its name, Terra Mitica is an amusement park that aims to replicate the ancient world. In here, you can visit Egypt, Siberia and Rome using different fun rides. Some of its popular amenities include the Titanide and SynKope. There are even exhilarating rides wherein you will be launched up in the air at more than 60 kilometers an hour while being rocked up and down.

2. Isla Magica, Seville

This amusement park first opened its doors back in 1997. It has seven theme parks that are scattered around the nearby lake. Isla Magica highlights the rich history and culture of the country. Each of their rides tells great tales about the various adventures that the Spanish explorers had while travelling to the New World.

Some of their themed areas include El Dorado, the Fountain of Youth, Amazonia, and a whole lot more. There are roller coasters, Ferris wheels, games and various activities that the little ones will definitely enjoy. There is also a cinema house that features popular documentaries and Spanish films.

3. Sioux City, Gran Canaria

Sioux City is a popular theme park for people who love to go back in time and revisit the good old days when Cowboys ruled over the Wild West. Unlike other amusement parks in the country, this one has fewer roller coasters. However, that does not mean that it is entirely boring and bland. In fact, you will definitely enjoy it more because of the various action-packed performances courtesy of the stunt actors. In addition, the kids can also have a taste of the Wild West by dressing up as cowboys or Indians.

4. Port Aventura – Salou, Tarragona

The Port Aventura theme park can be found in the southern side of Barcelona. This makes the place more accessible because there are railroads and buses that are available in this area. This amusement park is owned by the Universal Mediterranean Resort. Its neighboring establishments include the Costa Caribe Aquapark and El Paso.

In Port Aventura, you will have the opportunity to explore vast exotic lands that are found around the world. Your journey will begin in Spain's Cataluña region. Then, you will traverse the lands of Polynesia and learn more about the country's exciting folklore. Afterwards, you will jump to China and visit its great wall. Your final destination will be the rugged plains of the Wild West in America.

Aside from the fun anecdotes, there are also live performances and other forms of entertainment that greatly represent the culture of the featured country. In addition, there are also bars, restaurants, and shops that you can visit.

5. Warner Brothers Movie World, Madrid

This amusement park is separated into different regions such as the Superheroes World, or the Old West Territory. Each area has its very own themed rides and attractions that can be greatly enjoyed by both adults and kids. Warner Brothers Movie World is perfect for movie buffs that are searching for alternative ways to enjoy the films that they loved. There are so many movies that are featured in this theme park so you will not have a hard time enjoying the wonders of this place.

6. Parque de Atracciones de Madrid

Located in the heart of the Spanish capital, the Parque de Atracciones de Madrid is home to 40 exhilarating rides that the family will definitely love.

Some of its legendary rides include the Abismo and Tornado roller coasters. They have such frightful names because these rides have blazing speeds of 100 kilometers per hour. In addition, these roller coasters will also hurl you across nauseating loops and steep turns.

La Lanzadera, on the other hand, is another popular attraction that will drop unwary passengers from a 63 meter free fall in just three seconds. Another ride that you should try is Las Cadenas. It is a giant swing that is attached to long chains and flies around in wide arcs.

Travel Guide Box Set #20: The Best of Spain for Tourists + The Best of Beautiful Greece for Tourists + The Best of Italy for Tourists + The Best of Beautiful Germany for Tourists + The Best of Beautiful France for Tourists

Conclusion

Thank you again for purchasing this book!

I hope this book was able to help you to discover the best travel destinations that the country has to offer.

The next step is to relax and enjoy your vacation in Spain.

Finally, if you enjoyed this book, please take the time to share your thoughts and post a review on Amazon. We do our best to reach out to readers and provide the best value we can. Your positive review will help us achieve that. It'd be greatly appreciated!

Thank you and good luck!

Book 2:
The Best Of Beautiful Greece for Tourists
BY GETAWAY GUIDES

The Ultimate Guide for Greece's Sites, Restaurants, Shopping, and Beaches for Tourists!

Travel Guide Box Set #20: The Best of Spain for Tourists + The Best of Beautiful Greece for Tourists + The Best of Italy for Tourists + The Best of Beautiful Germany for Tourists + The Best of Beautiful France for Tourists

Copyright 2014 by Getaway Guides - All rights reserved.

In no way is it legal to reproduce, duplicate, or transmit any part of this document in either electronic means or in printed format. Recording of this publication is strictly prohibited and any storage of this document is not allowed unless with written permission from the publisher. All rights reserved.

Travel Guide Box Set #20: The Best of Spain for Tourists + The Best of Beautiful Greece for Tourists + The Best of Italy for Tourists + The Best of Beautiful Germany for Tourists + The Best of Beautiful France for Tourists

Table Of Contents

Introduction **23**

Chapter 1   Locating Greece 24

Chapter 2   Ancient Sites in Greece 25

Chapter 3   Greek Dining Experience 29

Chapter 4   Shopping in Greece 32

Chapter 5   Greece's Famous Beaches 34

Conclusion **37**

Travel Guide Box Set #20: The Best of Spain for Tourists + The Best of Beautiful Greece for Tourists + The Best of Italy for Tourists + The Best of Beautiful Germany for Tourists + The Best of Beautiful France for Tourists

Introduction

I want to thank you and congratulate you for purchasing the book, *"The Best Of Beautiful Greece for Tourists: The Ultimate Guide for Greece's Sites, Restaurants, Shopping, and Beaches for Tourists!"*

This book contains a collection of sites and places to see when in Greece. This book aims to help you make the most out of your visit to enchanting Greece. Rich in ancient culture with a busy modern urban lifestyle, Greece offers lots of places to see and experience. With this book, you will learn all the popular places to go. Also, discover the best-kept secret places that will make a tour in Greece even more interesting, fun, and memorable.

Read this book to help you prepare better for a trip to Greece.

Thanks again for purchasing this book, I hope you enjoy it!

Travel Guide Box Set #20: The Best of Spain for Tourists + The Best of Beautiful Greece for Tourists + The Best of Italy for Tourists + The Best of Beautiful Germany for Tourists + The Best of Beautiful France for Tourists

Chapter 1 Locating Greece

Greece has always had a charm that enchanted the world since the ancient times. The birthplace of Greek mythology, ancient Greek civilization, and Greek philosophy, society and culture, this country has greatly influenced both the ancient and the modern world.

This country is also one of the most popular tourist destinations in the world. It has numerous ruins and archeological sites, which gave modern societies a glimpse of how complex and advanced Ancient Greek society really was. These were proof that they had far more superior technologies and way of living than most parts of the world during the ancient times. Some of these sites are believed to be where Greek myths came to life. Tourists and academics alike flock to this country to study and marvel at these ancient sites.

Another attraction in Greece is the food experience. Traditional Greek cuisine is world-renowned for its exotic, exciting, and interesting array of food flavors, tastes, and textures. From salads and dips to main courses and desserts, the Greek gastronomic experience is an adventure all its own.

Because of its location in the Mediterranean, Greece is also host to some of the world's most wonderful beaches. Greece is truly blessed with pristine waters and fine beaches, the best that nature can give.

Location and Geography

Greece is officially known as The Hellenic Republic. It is at the southernmost tip of the European mainland. Greece is actually composed of over 3,000 islands, scattered on the eastern portion of the Mediterranean Sea. The main Greek island is roughly the size of state of New York or of England with an area measuring 131.940 square kilometers. It is bordered by Turkey, Albania, Bulgaria, and the Former Yugoslav Republic of Macedonia.

The capital and largest city of Greece is Athens. This is also where the country's main port, Piraeus, is situated.

Greece's time zone is in the GMT+2. The climate is typical of the Mediterranean- mild winters and warm, dry summers.

The country is bordered on the north by Albania, Bulgaria and Macedonia. This makes it more part of the Balkans when considering its geographic location. However, Greece is still considered as part of Western Europe. Turkey lies on the northeastern border of the country. Many other Greek islands are actually closer to Turkey than to the Greek main island. The island of Crete lies in the south, close to Libya and Egypt. By ship, one can go from Crete to these neighboring countries in just 2 days.

Travel Guide Box Set #20: The Best of Spain for Tourists + The Best of Beautiful Greece for Tourists + The Best of Italy for Tourists + The Best of Beautiful Germany for Tourists + The Best of Beautiful France for Tourists

Chapter 2 Ancient Greek Sites

The lure of Greece nowadays is mainly because of its ancient sites. Archeologists and tourists alike often flock to Greece to study and marvel at the ruins of bygone civilizations. Adding to the antiquities of these sites is their association with the many scenes in Greek mythology. Sites include the temple of the Greek gods and ruins of ancient Greek civilizations, which are largely believed to be the kingdoms described in many Greek epics such as the Odyssey.

Acropolis

This is the most famous ancient tourist site in the whole of Greece. It has become the very testament of what ancient Greece stood for. It became a symbol of Greece as a world power, whose influence reached all corners of the globe and across time.

It is a citadel built on top of a rocky hillside that overlooks the entire city of Athens. It is composed of several ancient buildings. Most were constructed during the 5th century BC. The popular among the buildings is the Parthenon, a temple dedicated to the city (and the country's) patron, the Greek goddess of wisdom, Athena. Other buildings with equally historic significance and great architectural importance are the Erechtheion, temple of Athena Nike, and the Propylaia.

Nemea

The Nemea is located in the Peloponnese. It is a recently restored ancient Greek structure. It has a beautiful and breathtaking stadium, an impressive museum and a picnic area with a fantastic view of the classic Doric temple. The columns are currently being restored by a team of archeologists. Only 3 of the original thousand-years-old columns still stand. All the other columns that now stand in the temple are newly reconstructed as a part of an ambitious project to restore the ancient grandeur of the Nemea. Efforts at present are on the restoration of the north façade of the temple.

Olympia

The Olympia is located in the Peloponnese. This is where the Olympic Games began. It is a complex of massive temples interspersed with groves of trees that provide good shade.

Delphi

Located in Central Greece, Delphi is where the Oracle was found. It was said that the Oracle at Delphi gave prophesies. In those times, people far and wide would travel just to seek counsel from the Oracle before going on a journey, before making important decisions, and when planning for war.

Travel Guide Box Set #20: The Best of Spain for Tourists + The Best of Beautiful Greece for Tourists + The Best of Italy for Tourists + The Best of Beautiful Germany for Tourists + The Best of Beautiful France for Tourists

Delphi was dedicated to the Greek sun god Apollo. It was built on top of mountain slopes that overlook the sea and a grove of olive trees. The view from Delphi is truly breathtaking, making it one of the most stunning ancient sites in the whole of Greece. Tourists especially flock to see the famous ruins of the Treasury of the Athenians and the Temple of Apollo. In the ancient times, Delphi was considered as the center of the Earth, from which past, present, and future were forged. The place is expansive, and tourists may need to take a longer time to explore the entire site. Some opt to take one of the scheduled tours in order to see only the highlights of Delphi to save time.

Knossos

This ancient Greek site is located in Crete. It was a prosperous city that served as the center of the ancient Minoan civilization. Tourists are treated to a thrilling mix of both real archaeological artifacts and a pervading sense of legends of myths. According to Greek legend, this was where King Minos lived and ruled over the most powerful and richest cities of the Minoan civilization. He had a complex maze built and placed the Minotaur, a beast that was half-man and half-bull, in it. Anyone who entered the maze never got out—everyone except the mortal hero Theseus. With the help of the king's daughter Ariadne, Theseus was able to kill the Minotaur and successfully make his way through the maze. This is also where the story of father and son Daedalus and Icarus attempted their escape from the city by flying. According to the legend, the inventor Daedalus was said to have designed and developed the famous labyrinth. Icarus was his son who flew too close to the sun, which caused the wax on his wings to melt. He then plunged into the sea and tragically died.

The ruins do show an elaborate and unending maze, with numerous rooms, levels, corridors, stairways and frescoed walls. This site is very popular among tourists. It is advisable to get a guidebook of the maze to avoid getting lost or going in circles. The ruins are indeed a labyrinth full of confusing twists and turns. Aside from the maze, the Palace of Knossos, where King Minos lived is also a notable attraction. It can get a little crowded, especially at the peak of the tourist season.

Delos

Delos is a tiny isle at the center of the Cyclades. It is 2 miles (3.2 kilometers) off the coast of Mykonos. The Ancient Greeks considered this small isle as the spiritual center of the Cyclades and treated it as the holiest sanctuary in all of Greece. There are extensive remains of ancient temples and religious structures, attesting to its importance in the spiritual aspect of Ancient Greece.

Most tours allot 3 hours to explore the island. However, due to the wealth of archeological finds, it may take more than the allotted time to appreciate this site fully.

Travel Guide Box Set #20: The Best of Spain for Tourists + The Best of Beautiful Greece for Tourists + The Best of Italy for Tourists + The Best of Beautiful Germany for Tourists + The Best of Beautiful France for Tourists

Vergina

This is situated in Northern Greece. It has a museum complex superbly designed, where it is believed to be where the tomb of Philip of Macedon used to lie. Philip was the father of Alexander the Great. Near the museum is an expansive burial site, housing more than 300 burial mounds. The mounds stretch across the Macedonian plain for miles.

Akrotiri

The Akrotiri is a lesser-known ancient site. It is located on the island of Santorini. The site was closed to tourists when one of the roofs collapsed several years ago. It has been recently opened and now open for sightseeing.

Akrotiri is an ancient city that some believe to be similar to that of the fabled Pompeii in Italy, but older by 2,000 years. It was destroyed by volcanic eruption, buried under layers of volcanic ash and pyroclastic material. The ancient city was spectacularly preserved. The ruins showed just how advanced and sophisticated this ancient society was compared to contemporary societies at the time. The 2 to 3 storey buildings with ornate frescoes revealed how advanced these people's lives were in those days. The everyday materials like pottery and furniture indicated how complex their culture and society were already. Because of all these, some were led to believe that Akrotiri is actually the lost city of Atlantis.

Epidaurus

Epidaurus is one of the best ancient places to visit when in Greece. This tourist site attracts a lot of visitors. It tends to get crowded during peak tourist season. Still, the trip will be worth it as one gets treated to a one of a kind experience.

One will find the ruins of an ancient Greek theater in this site. It is a very expansive structure, originally built to accommodate 15,000 people at once. Epidaurus was once a city with a bustling, complex society more advanced than other societies in the world during its time. This well-preserved 2,000-year-old city is set over 3 levels, offering a glimpse of how life was in ancient Greece.

Mystras

This is a medieval Greek city built on top of a stunning hillside landscape. One can see and study old palaces, houses, churches and streets. There are also monasteries with awe-inspiring frescoes. A large and imposing castle looms above, perched on the summit of the hill.

Mystras has a very intriguing history. According to legend, sometime in the 18th century, the entire town was abandoned in haste. It looked as if everyone dropped everything and left at a moment's notice. Visitors entering the town say that the experience is like stepping back in time. The entire city looked as if all the inhabitants just left the day before.

Travel Guide Box Set #20: The Best of Spain for Tourists + The Best of Beautiful Greece for Tourists + The Best of Italy for Tourists + The Best of Beautiful Germany for Tourists + The Best of Beautiful France for Tourists

Mycenae

Mycenae was the center of the ancient Mycenaean civilization. It is found in the Peloponnese. At the height of the Mycenaean civilization, this city had been one of Ancient Greece's most important cities. This was once believed to be the site of Troy, the city in the Greek epic that started the Trojan War after their prince abducted Queen Helena. This is where the stories of Agamemnon, Achilles and the others believed to have truly happened.

Today, the ancient city of Mycenae is a well-preserved archeological site. Notable to explore within this ancient site are the Terraced Palace, the Lion's Gate, the fortified walls, and the famous tomb of Agamemnon.

Grandmasters' Palace

The Grandmasters Palace can be visited in the island of Rhodes. This is a magnificent medieval fortress, used in the past by the Knights Hospitaller. The Knights were religious warriors that went on crusades. They were famous in those days for their immense power and influence over a large part of Europe during the early medieval period.

Today, the castle has been converted into a museum. It has several exhibits that cover everything from the period of early Christianity until the time of the Ottoman conquest. The castle itself is great to explore, although the restorations done were part-19th century. The massive battlements are very impressive and give off a medieval vibe. It is highly recommended for tourist exploration.

Meteora

Meteora was built in 14th century. It served to provide shelter to the Turks that invaded the Greeks in the 14th and 15th centuries.

Meteora is one of the most astonishing sites in Greece. It was a complex of monasteries that were built precariously on top of rocky outcroppings. The monasteries seemed to dangle above the ground for hundreds of feet. The sight is astounding and is no wonder among the must-see destinations in Greece.

Temple of Hephaestus

The Temple of Hephaestus is often overlooked. It is overshadowed by nearby towering and more famous Parthenon. This site is smaller than the Parthenon but is much better preserved. It is also less crowded and quieter. This is also one of the best temples in the entire Greek peninsula.

Travel Guide Box Set #20: The Best of Spain for Tourists + The Best of Beautiful Greece for Tourists + The Best of Italy for Tourists + The Best of Beautiful Germany for Tourists + The Best of Beautiful France for Tourists

Chapter 3 Greek Dining Experience

Greek dishes are known all over the world. It is among the healthiest fare, with a wealth of fresh vegetables, cheeses and healthy olive oils. When in Greece, there are different restaurants that serve special dishes. Here's a guide to understand Greek restaurant names.

Estiatorio

This restaurant serves foods cooked in a *magerefta* or traditional oven. Some *estiatoria* also serve grilled foods called *tis oras*, salads, fish, and *mezedes* or appetizers. These are open day and night, but most are only open during the day.

Good ones to check are the Byzantino and Plaka Taverna. These *estiatoria* are located side by side on Kydatheneon Street, in the Plaka. These 2 are within the touristdense centers and offer an array of different fares like grilled meats (taverna-fare) and fish (psaro taverna-fare). A more traditional *estiatorio* is the Iepirus Restaurant located at the meat market, also at the Plaka. It is open daily, 24 hours and serves podi and patsa. Diros and Delphi, located near Syntagma are high-end *estiatoria*. Kalofagon Taverna in Hora is an *oinozythestiatoriaon*, or a wine and hot food restaurant.

Psistaria

A *psistaria* is a restaurant that serves grilled food. Specialties include *kokoretsi*, spit-roast lamb, grilled or rotisserie chicken and steaks. It also serves appetizers and salads. *Psistarias* are more common outside the city, where there are lots of spaces for the some. Good places to try include Vari (town between Varkiza and Voula), Mount Parnitha and Kalivia (past the airport going to Lavrion). The Pat Cute in Platia Victoria is a fancy psistaria-souvlaki store.

Taverna

This type of restaurant offers a smaller menu. Dishes are mostly for nighttime long meals, when there are lots of conversation and wine. It is commonly known that anything can happen in a taverna. It is not surprising for a quiet taverna to suddenly erupt into singing, dancing, and even plate smashing. It is not a brawl, but rather, a boisterous, fun, impromptu party. Most tavernas within the city have changed into restaurants to cater to tourists. Decent and traditional tavernas are more likely to be seen in neighborhoods like Goudi.

A few real tavernas still operate near central Athens. There is the *Taverna Psiri* located on Agios Dimitrios Street and *To Steki Tou Elia* located next to the tracks in Thission. There is also the *Saita* right in the Plaka, a basement tavern that opens only during the winter. This shop specializes in fried cod, locally known as *bakaliaro*.

Psaro tavernas

Fish tavernas or *psaro tavernas* are often found by the sea and on the islands. Some are found right in Athens. These places can get festive and crowded in the summer and on Sundays. People generally spend time here from 2 in the afternoon until the evenings. Customers can buy fresh fish by the gram or kilo. There are also lots of appetizers, meat and vegetable dishes. Psaro tavernas in Athens are generally located around Anagenessios Square, towards Kessariani. More fish tavernas can be found along the coast.

Ouzerie and Mezedopoulions

These restaurants specialize in dishes eaten with ouzo which is a Greek liquor flavored with anise. Those found in Psiri are far from traditional quiet ouzeries. These have electronic music, more like a bar.

The traditional and good ones are more likely to be found in towns like Thessaloniki and Volos. Good traditional ouzeries can also be found in islands like Lesvos. It harder t o find a good ouzerie in Athens. Quiet and decent ones can be found in the Plaka (the To Kafeneon), Psiri (Naxos or Evi) and Monastiraki (To Hani Ton Othona). The ouzeries found by the sea often offer fish and other local dishes and also includes some popular dishes from all around Greece.

Tsipuradiko

This is an ouzerie that serves Tsipuro instead of ouzo. A tsipuro is a strong liquor like ouzo but without the flavor of anise.

Fournos

These are Greek bakeries that sell a huge assortment of baked goods. This includes loaves of bread, cheese pie (tiropitas), spinach pie (spanakopitas), leek pie (prasatopita), onion pie (kremedopitas), zucchini pie (kolokithopita), chicken pie (kotopita), eggplant pie (melitzanitopita), meat pie (kreatopita), kasseri meat pie (kaseritopita) and zerotopita or tipatopita (pies with no fillings).

The one of the best and most famous fournos is Ariston, located on Voulis Street, 2 blocks away from Syntagma Square.

Souvlaki

This type of food shop sells gyro and kebabs, which are very popular with tourists. Very popular souvlaki shops that tourists frequent are found in Athens, particularly at the end of Metropolis Street.

Other notable Restaurants all over Greece

Spondi

Award-winning restaurant and considered the best place to dine in Athens. It boasts of exceptional cuisine in a beautiful 19th century town house, complete with a stone courtyard surrounded with bougainvilleas. The service is also excellent.

Fish Taverna Tkis to Limeni

Located in Limeni, Mani, Peloponnese, this fish tavern gives visitors an authentic open-air fish tavern experience. It serves fresh fish, which are still swimming in underwater cages just before they are cooked.

Selene

This is the best restaurant in Santorini, Cyclades. It used to be in Fira and moved to Pyrgos. They feature innovations and new twists to traditional Greek dishes.

Travel Guide Box Set #20: The Best of Spain for Tourists + The Best of Beautiful Greece for Tourists + The Best of Italy for Tourists + The Best of Beautiful Germany for Tourists + The Best of Beautiful France for Tourists

Chapter 4 Shopping Adventure in Greece

Greece also has abundant shops that cater to the different preferences. There are specialty shops that offer unique Greek merchandise, from traditional crafts to modern souvenir items.

Greek Arts & Crafts

For those who are seeking to buy traditional Greek arts and crafts, the needlework is the most notable. It can be purchased in many shops all over Greece. Anyone can buy high quality needlework in just about any shop that offers these crafts. The best shops are found in Rhodes, Crete and Skyros.

Athens also has 2 good places to shop for traditional arts and crafts. One is The Center of Hellenic Tradition located at 59 Mitropoleos and 36 Pandrossou. This shop offers an array of prints, woodcarvings and ceramics. A stunning view of the Acropolis can also be gleamed from the shop. The other is the National Welfare Organization located at 6 Ipatias and Apollonos. It has a large collection of exceptional ceramic and copper work. It also offers items made by Greek village women such as silk embroidery and hand-loomed rugs.

Greek Jewelry

Jewelry is sold in Greece almost everywhere. Most of the retail stores offer jewelry, so it is easy for anyone to make some purchases. Greek jewelry is not much different from the ones sold elsewhere around the world. There is no distinct Greek jewelry design.

However, despite the lack of authentic and truly Greek jewelry design, the craftsmanship is truly remarkable. A number of jewelers in Athens are internationally recognized for outstanding craftsmanship. These include major jewelers like Zolotas and LALAoUNis.

For local artisan work, check the jewelry shops in northwest Greece, Ionnina, Crete and Chania. The pieces are sophisticated and worth the trip. Items that are more in tuned with tourist preferences can be found in the numerous stores in the islands of Santorini, Paros, Hydra, Skiathos, Rhodes and Mykonos. Jewelry pieces are made by local jewelers.

Weavings and Rugs

A good array of rugs and woven materials are also available in different shops around Greece. The best ones are found in Crete, which also has the widest array of these items. There are also some unique textiles offered in Metsovo. For those interested in rag rugs, there are numerous small shops that sell *kourouloudes* across the Peloponnese.

Woodcraft

When looking for wooden crafts, the best place to go to is Corfu. This is considered as Greece's center for products made of olive wood. Items include a good collection of utensils, various bowls, and carving boards. Another place with a good collection of woodworks is Rethymnon, Crete.

Another good place to shop for wood is in the villages of Arcadia in the Peloponnese, where there are various utensils and woodcarvings. Woodcarving traditions are also still alive in the islands of Mitilini, Syros, Paros and Chios.

Ecclesiastical Books, Icons and Other Religious Artifacts

For people who wish to shop for religious merchandise, a good place to visit is the streets of the Metropolitan in Athens, in the area of the Greek Orthodox Cathedral. There is an assortment of candles, votive offerings, and reproductions of different religious icons.

When in Thessaloniki, visit the Apostolic Diakonta. This shop has a large collection of different religious items. Important religious shrines also sell religious items, like in Panagia Evangelista on Tinos. Convents and monasteries throughout Greece sell a variety of religious items such as reproductions of religious icons. The monasteries in Meteora are among those that sell such items. The Petrakis couple living in Elounda, situated on the island of Crete, is internationally sought for their paintings of traditional icons.

Natural Products

Natural, organic products are now being offered in retail stores all over Greece. Items include natural produce such as jams, honey, and olive oil. They also offer cosmetics made from all natural and organic ingredients.

Great food products are also available in various places. The best ones are those found in shops, delis and groceries with the labels Stater, Peloponnese, Milelia, Yiam, Gaea and Nefeli.

Travel Guide Box Set #20: The Best of Spain for Tourists + The Best of Beautiful Greece for Tourists + The Best of Italy for Tourists + The Best of Beautiful Germany for Tourists + The Best of Beautiful France for Tourists

Chapter 5 Enjoying the Beach, Greek-Style

Aside from a rich history, culture and tradition, Greece is also gifted in the beauty of nature. From imposing and picturesque mountains and pristine blue seas, Greece seems to have it all. The beaches abound in Greece. All are amazing and stunning, with clear blue waters and pure white sand. Some have nearby magnificent rock formations that add to the beauty of the seaside. People all over the world flock to Greece to enjoy the pure beauty and wonder of nature by the beach.

Arvanitia

Situated in Nafplion, Peloponnese, the Arvinita is a little municipal beach. It is a convenient place to relax after a tiring day spent sightseeing. It can be quick rest stop in between visits to the ruins in Mycenae and watching a play in Epidaurus. Just drop by, swim and relax by the beach. When good to go, head over to the many handy showers and changing rooms before continuing with visits to other Greek attractions.

Chrissi Akti and Santa Maria

These beaches are found in Paros, Cyclades. It is highly recommended for beachgoers who love water sports. Chrissi Akti and Santa Maria's main attraction is windsurfing. It is an excellent location for this water sport as the winds are reliable to give good surfing. People who are more on the relaxed side have plenty to watch while lounging by the beach. There are also a lot of restaurants and cafes by the beachside to serve a variety of snacks and refreshments.

Paradise

Paradise is famous for its beach parties. The revelries are known to get wild and can go on for most of the night and well into the wee hours of the morning. Paradise is an extensive complex built along the beach in Mykonos, Cyclades. It has a tavern, a bar, souvenir shops and changing rooms. This is one beach to see and be seen. People from around the world, including Greek locals and celebrities spend time under the sun, to show off.

Lalaria

Lalaria beach is located in Skiathos, Sporades. The beach is a gleaming white-pebbled one. The aquamarine water is very clear one can almost see the bottom of the sea. Out in the water are white limestone cliffs. These cliffs have natural arches, shaped by wind and water over centuries. The whole area is nature at its most unspoiled state.

Myrtos

Myrtos is a remote beach in Kefalonia, Ionian Islands. It is a sand-pebbled beach, with clear blue waters. This isolated beach has attracted numerous tourists for years. The place offers very limited refreshments. When visiting Myrtos, it is best to bring a picnic. The setting is actually a perfect place to spread a blanket and have a simple picnic while enjoying the view.

Vroulidia

This is a cliff-rimmed cove with gleaming white sand. It is on a remote location at Northeastern Aegean, on the southern tip of an island called Hios. This is a small beach with exquisite setting. The coast is rocky, which partly covers the beach, making it partly hidden and away from crowds.

Katergo

This is a private beach haven and one of the most famous ones in Folegandros. It is known for its emerald green, crystal clear waters. The beach is long and pebbled. The location is remote enough to offer solitude and repose. It can be reached either by boat or by a 1-hour hike from Livadi. People who plan to go to Katergo should bring food and water. This beach is non-organized—no changing rooms, restaurants, and cafes.

This beach used to be a mining area for haematite. The name actually meant galley, referring to the mines.

Agrari

This beach is a famous for its clothes-optional culture. It is medium-sized beach of pebbly sand. The beach is semi-organized, with strewn umbrellas and sun beds available for rent to beach goers. There is also a beach ba, a hotel, a water sports area and a traditional tavern nearby.

This beach attracts a mix of Greeks and tourists. It can be reached by motorbike or car. There are no direct bus rides to the Agrari. The way to the beach is a hill that provides stunning view from the top. The beach is also accessible by boat from Ornos bay or Platis Gialos, or by foot if coming from nearby Elia Beach.

Agia Anna

The Agia Anna beach is small and hidden, not far from the more famous Kalafatis. The name came from the tiny chapel of St. Anna nearby, where locals flock to light prayer candles.

This beach is a good alternative to the more crowded beaches in the southern part of Greece. Agia Anna beach is protected from strong winds. Visitors get a glimpse of traditional Greek fishing village life. Along the beach are several fish tavernas, fishermen's houses and a boat launch. There are a few umbrellas and sun beds for rent, with a hotel, rooms, tavernas and restaurants.

In the horizon is the Divounia, which are 2 rocky hills that seem to float in the sea. The name means 2 mountains, or locally known as Aphrodite's tits.

Travel Guide Box Set #20: The Best of Spain for Tourists + The Best of Beautiful Greece for Tourists + The Best of Italy for Tourists + The Best of Beautiful Germany for Tourists + The Best of Beautiful France for Tourists

The beach can be reached by car, local bus service or motorbike.

Ornos Beach

This is a family friendly beach located just 2 kilometers away from Mykonos town. It is located on the southwest of Mykonos Island. It is easily accessed by a regular bus service and a boat service to Delos and Rhenia islands.

The sandy beach is very organized. There are several sun beds and umbrellas for rent. The beach is also surrounded by several villas, hotels and apartments. There are also several cafes, bars, restaurants and tavernas. There are also groceries, butcher's shops, pharmacies, supermarkets, and all kinds of shops.

Kalafatis

One of the more famous beaches in Greece, the Kalafatis is known for its water sports, particularly wind surfing. There is also a dive center nearby. The beach also has a beach volley court and a water sports area.

Nearby are a number of apartments, rooms for rent and hotels. A taverna and a restaurant by the beach serve refreshments.

Along the beach are a number of umbrellas and sun beds for rent. There is also ample space to spread a beach towel and lie basking under the sun. Kalafatis beach is actually next to the last beach in the southern tip of Mykonos island. It can be accessed by motorbike, rental car, or public transport (regular bus service).

Elafonisi

This is a very small and uninhabited islet in Crete. It is located on the edge of a lagoon, scenic for its stunning turquoise waters. The sand is pinky-white, that extends and joins the warm and clear waters of the lagoon. The water is shallow enough for wading. While this place is remote, it can get a little crowded during the peak tourist season.

Travel Guide Box Set #20: The Best of Spain for Tourists + The Best of Beautiful Greece for Tourists + The Best of Italy for Tourists + The Best of Beautiful Germany for Tourists + The Best of Beautiful France for Tourists

Conclusion

Thank you again for purchasing this book!

I hope this book was able to help you know what places to visit in Greece. Travelling is an adventure, but knowing what the destination has to offer can help you in planning your itinerary. It also makes sure you don't miss out on all the attractions that Greece has to offer.

The next step is to start planning a trip to Greece today! Whether it's with your family, friends, or your special someone, a Greek vacation will be a truly unforgettable experience!

Finally, if you enjoyed this book, please take the time to share your thoughts and post a review on Amazon. We do our best to reach out to readers and provide the best value we can. Your positive review will help us achieve that. It'd be greatly appreciated!

Thank you and good luck!

Book 3:
The Best of Italy for Tourists
BY GETAWAT GUIDES

The Ultimate Guide of Italy's Sites, Restaurants, Shopping and Beaches for Tourists!

Travel Guide Box Set #20: The Best of Spain for Tourists + The Best of Beautiful Greece for Tourists + The Best of Italy for Tourists + The Best of Beautiful Germany for Tourists + The Best of Beautiful France for Tourists

Copyright 2014 by Getaway Guides - All rights reserved.

In no way is it legal to reproduce, duplicate, or transmit any part of this document in either electronic means or in printed format. Recording of this publication is strictly prohibited and any storage of this document is not allowed unless with written permission from the publisher. All rights reserved.

Travel Guide Box Set #20: The Best of Spain for Tourists + The Best of Beautiful Greece for Tourists + The Best of Italy for Tourists + The Best of Beautiful Germany for Tourists + The Best of Beautiful France for Tourists

Table Of Contents

Introduction 41

Chapter 1: The Passion for Italy 42

Chapter 2: The Sicilian Surprise 45

Chapter 3: The Florentine Fulfillment 49

Chapter 4: The Milan Mania 52

Chapter 5: The Roman Resplendence 54

Chapter 6: The Venetian Venture 57

Conclusion 59

Travel Guide Box Set #20: The Best of Spain for Tourists + The Best of Beautiful Greece for Tourists + The Best of Italy for Tourists + The Best of Beautiful Germany for Tourists + The Best of Beautiful France for Tourists

Introduction

I want to thank you and congratulate you for purchasing the book, *"The Best of Italy for Tourists: The Ultimate Guide of Italy's Sites, Restaurants, Shopping and Beaches for Tourists!"*.

This book contains proven steps and strategies on how to enjoy a trip to Italy without adopting another's itinerary or travel plans.

Unlike other books which tend to provide readers with specific instructions on how to do things as well as detailed descriptions of places which may prove inadequate as they do not give justice to the indescribable account of the actual sight and lessen one's actual appreciation of the experience, this book merely contains suggestions and aims to leave plenty to one's imagination and powers of discretion in order to enable him to enjoy his travels by making his own adventure.

Thanks again for purchasing this book, I hope you enjoy it!

Travel Guide Box Set #20: The Best of Spain for Tourists + The Best of Beautiful Greece for Tourists + The Best of Italy for Tourists + The Best of Beautiful Germany for Tourists + The Best of Beautiful France for Tourists

Chapter 1 The Passion for Italy

The Passion for Italy

Recent data on international tourism from the United Nations World Tourism Organization and the World Bank reveal that Italy ranks fifth as the most popular tourist destination in the world with more than 46 million tourists annually generating revenues of approximately €136 billion or an equivalent of more than 180 billion US dollars.

In spite of its small boot-shaped appearance amid its huge neighbors in the world map, Italy has been known for its greatness throughout the centuries. Aside from conceiving immensely satisfying food like pasta, pizza and a wide variety of mouth-watering desserts, Italy is known for its contributions in many fields which have brought about progress and continue to influence human development. Paying homage to many of the great names that enriched civilization is one of the reasons why many tourists consider it as their favorite destination with great passion.

Film

In film alone, Italy has produced great names like actors Terence Hill (born Mario Girotti) who was popular for his action and western films with co-actor Bud Spencer, Rudolph Valentino, known as the "Great Lover" in the early 20s, model-actresses Sophia Loren, Monica Bellucci and Isabella Rossellini as well as internationally renowned directors like Gianni Amelio (for The Stolen Children), Bernardo Bertolucci (for Last Tango in Paris) and Franco Zeffirelli (for his adaptations of some of Shakespeare's works) who have all earned the admiration of many.

Architecture

The grandeur in most of its structures which is responsible for drawing tourists every year is owed to renowned architects such as Vitruvius, Guglielmo Agnelli, Pietro Baseggio, Bartolomeo Bon, Diotisalvi (for the Baptistry of Pisa), Donato Bramante, who conceptualized the contemporary St. Peter's Basilica, Filippo Brunelleschi, for the dome of the Florence Cathedral, Nicola Salvi, for the Trevi Fountain in Rome, Carlo Rossi, Francesco Sabatini, 9-time top prize winner of Caompasso d'Oro for industrial design Achille Castiglioni, multi-awarded Ignazio Gardella, Luigi Moretti and Mario Bellini.

Gastronomy

Similarly, the worldwide distinction bestowed on Italian cuisine can be attributed to experts like Martino da Como, whose work became the standard for Italian cooking, Pellegrino Artusi, who established genuine Italian cuisine uniting all regions of Italy and Carlo Petrini, who founded the Slow Food movement in the mid-80s against fastfood chains like McDonald's, which became a significant influence around the world.

Geography

The discovery of other lands was likewise led by great Italian explorers like Giovanni Caboto, also known as John Cabot, who discovered the mainland of Northern America; Cristoforo Colombo whom everyone popularly known as Christopher Columbus who discovered America; Antonio Pigafetta, who circumnavigated the world together with Magellan and discovered some lands in the east; Marco Polo, who was famous for his commercial exchanges with Central Asia and China; Amerigo Vespucci, who discovered of the Amazon River and from whom America derives its name and Romolo Gessi, who was responsible for freeing thousands of slaves in his expeditions in Africa and Sudan.

Political History

Moreover, early Italian statesmen like Lucius Aemilius Paullus Macedonicus, Scipio Africanus, Mark Antony, Augustus, Qunitus Aurelius Symmacchus, Marcus Aurelius, Lucius Junius Brutus, Julius Caesar, Cicero, Germanicus, Marcus Licinius Crassus, Fabius Maximus, Pontius Pilate, Antonius Pius, Pompey, Titus Quinctius Flamininus, Quintus Sertorius and Marcus Vispanius Agrippa as well as modern politicians like Ottavio Piccolomini, Benito Mussolini, Antonio Di Pietro and Altiero Spinelli have brought about many changes that led to Italy's present state.

Roman Catholic Influences

By virtue of its position as one of the most influential religions in the world, the Roman Catholic Church also had some significant contributions through leaders like Popes Gregory I, II and VII, Pope Innocent III and Pope Leo II as well as those they deem as examples who have attained sainthood like St. Agatha of Sicily, Agnes of Rome, John Bosco, Catherine of Siena, St. Cecilia, St. Valentine, St. Anselm of Canterbury who founded Scholasticism, St. Thomas Aquinas (for Summa Theologica) and St. Francis of Assisi (founder of the Franciscan order).

Arts

One of the greatest contributions of Italy is in the realm of art. In music, some important names were Gregorio Allegri (for church music), Antonio Vivaldi (for violin music), composer Niccolo Paganini, Giuseppe Verdi (for opera) and internationally renowned operatic singers Cecilia Bartoli, Giovanni Martinelli, Andrea Bocelli and Luciano Pavarotti. In visual arts, some famous works were produced by painters and sculptors like Leonardo da Vinci, Michelangelo, Raphael, Donatello, Giovanni Paolo Panini, Giovanni Antonio Amadeo, Bartolomeo Ammanati, Lorenzo Bartolini, Pietro Cavallini, Cimabue, Duccio, Taddeo Gaddi and modern-day artist Alberto Burri who explored the use of waste materials in art.

Scientists and Inventors

In recognition of their discoveries and inventions, generations will never forget the great contributions of Galileo Galilei (founder of modern science and heliocentism), Guglielmo Marconi (inventor of wireless communication or radio and technology) Panfilo Castaldi (inventor of moveable type of printing) and Ottaviano Petrucci (for movable metal type and polyphonic music), Maria Gaetana Agnesi (in mathematics), Agostino Bassi (for contagious disease transmission), Enrico Fermi (for the first nuclear reactor), Luca Pacioli (for modern accounting methods) and Maria Montessori (for innovative educational methods).

Philosophy and Literature

Even at present, people continue to improve their minds with written works by famous Italian writers and philosophers such as Gaius Valerius Flaccus (for Argonautica), Horace, Virgil (for the Aeneid), Dante Alighieri (for The Divine Comedy), Giordano Bruno for his metaphysical works, Niccolo Machiavelli (for The Prince), Carlo Collodi (for Pinocchio) and Umberto Eco (for The Name of the Rose).

Sports

Italy has also been known to produce famous athletes and sportsmen such as Enzo Ferrari, 7-time world champion of Grand Prix motorcross Tony Cairoli, first World Champion of Formula One Giuseppe Farina, top scorer in FIFA world Cup and 1993 FIFA World Player of the Year Roberto Baggio and one of the greatest football players in Pele's list Paolo Rossi.

Entrepreneurs and designers

Other notable people patronized by many are entrepreneur Marcel Bich (co-founder of Bic company, internationally renowned for its popular Bic crystal pens); Giovanni Agnelli, founder the automobile company Fiat; perfume designer and Eau de Cologne inventor Johann Maria Farina; fashion designers Valentino, Pierre Cardin, Demenico Dolce, Stefano Gabbana, Salvatore Ferragamo, Franco Moschino, Mario and Miuccia Prada, Bruno Magli, Guccio Gucci, Gianni and Donatella Versace and Giorgio Armani.

Thus, as the seat of many things good and beautiful, Italy is among the places that one must see in order to believe and one can begin his journey with Sicily, Florence, Milan, Rome and Venice. On with the tour!

Travel Guide Box Set #20: The Best of Spain for Tourists + The Best of Beautiful Greece for Tourists + The Best of Italy for Tourists + The Best of Beautiful Germany for Tourists + The Best of Beautiful France for Tourists

Chapter 2 The Sicilian Surprise

The Sicilian Surprise

Unjustly depicted in movies as the headquarters of the Italian mafia, Sicily is otherwise a haven for tourists. As the biggest island in the Mediterranean Sea, it boasts of beautiful beaches, restaurants, shopping areas and some of the largest UNESCO heritage sites for historical landmarks.

Beaches

Awarded the Blue Flag which is a rating based on scientific standards given by the Foundation for Environmental Education which comprises of organizations from 59 countries across continents, six of its Beaches earned the distinction of being among the cleanest beaches in Europe in 2012. These are Porto Paolo, Pozzalo and Ispica, Fiumefreddo-Cottone, Spiaggia Biance and the Marina di Ragusa which is the most attractive among the cheaper beaches in Southern Sicily.

Other popular beaches are Mondello Beach, which provides not only accommodations in terms of mansions and villas but other water activities as well including boating and surfing; Aspra Beach, which is a small public beach known for having the best ice cream; Cefalu beach with long golden shores, easily accessible public showers and some areas with lifeguard watchtowers; Isola Delle Femmine Beach, which also a public beach west of Palermo known for its crystal clear waters and white sand.

Historic Sites

Some of the historic sites worth visiting in Sicily are the ancient tombs like the Catacombs of the Capuchins where preserved corpses from the 16th century are on exhibit and the Necropolis of Pantalica, which houses more than 5,000 ancient tombs carved in rock from 13-7BC; ancient churches like the Palermo Cathedral which was a place for royal coronations and burials and the Monreale Cathedral, a twelfth century church depicting Norman architecture characterized by rounded arches interlaced together and combined with Gothic and pointed Arab windows and heritage sites such as the inclomplete yet well-preserved Temple of Segesta, the Selinunte and Syracuse archaeological sites which contain ancient Greek ruins, the Valley of the Temples which houses the preserved vestiges of the Ancient Greek temples, the Taormina Ampitheater which was originally built by the Greeks and reconstructed by the Romans and the Villa Romana del Casale which contains the best Roman mosaics.

Restaurants

Sicily is known for its abundant variety of food. In order to facilitate one's eating choices, differentiating among terms may be useful. For instance, ristorantes are formal restaurants which are expected to be quite expensive, trattorias are less

Travel Guide Box Set #20: The Best of Spain for Tourists + The Best of Beautiful Greece for Tourists + The Best of Italy for Tourists + The Best of Beautiful Germany for Tourists + The Best of Beautiful France for Tourists

formal restaurants which may have meals which can cost as much as those served in restaurants, osterias are small restaurants which are less formal and cheaper than trattorias but offer limited menus, pizzerias are restaurants which specialize in various pizzas though may occasionally serve pasta and which are usually open only during the evening.

In general, restaurants require reservations and are open for lunch which starts at around 1:00pm and for dinner which starts at around 8pm except on Mondays. Trattorias, however, are often closed on Sundays and do not always serve dinner unlike pizzerias, which do serve dinner but do not serve lunch. Pollerias are small stands or shops which sell skewered chicken to go. Rosticcerias are stands that sell street food like rice balls and fries. Gelateria, from its root word, gelato, are ice cream parlors while pasticceria are pastry shops for the sweet toothed.

The more expensive restaurants in Sicily which serve meals above €40 or an equivalent of almost $55 and above are Trattoria Da Federico in Aci Trezza; Leon d'Oro in Agrigento; Don Ciccio in Bagheria; La Scala in Caltagirone; Ristorante Metro in Catania; Nangalarruni in Castelbuono; Ristorante del Golfo in Castellammare del Golfo; Il Consiglio di Sicilia in Donnalucata and Torre Marabino La Moresca in Ispica; Da Nino in Letojanni; La Madia in Licata; Boccaperta in Linguaglossa; I Bucanieri and Fior di Sale in Marsala; La Capinera, Il Barcaiolo, Da Giovanni, Pizzichella and Villa Sant'Andrea in Mazarro; Piccolo Casale in Milazzo; Torre d' Oriente, La Gazza Ladra and Fattoria Delle Torri in Modica; Da Calogero, Alle Terrazze and Michelin- starred Bye Bye Blues in Mondello; Bricco e Bacco in Monreale; Le Ularie and Borgo Alveria in Noto; Gigi Mangia, Sant'Andrea, Lo Scudiero, Cucina Papoff and Osteria dei Vespri in Palermo; Al Fogher, one of Sicily's best restaurants in Piazza Armerina; Trattoria al Faro Verde in Porticello and Da Vittorio in Porto Palo di Menfi; Duomo, Locanda Don Serafino, La Locandina and La Fenice in Ragusa; Donna Patrizia in Rosolini; Trattoria Scalo Grande and Ristorante Al Molino in Santa Maria La Scala; Acqua Pazza, Il Cavalluccio Marino and Il Barone in Santa Tecla; Pocho in San Vito Lo Capo; Hostaria Del Vicolo in Sciacca; the well-known Pomodoro in Scicli; Sakalleo in Scoglitti; Ristorante La Terraza in Scopello; Don Camillo, Regina Lucia, Porta Marina and Il Veliero in Siracusa; Michelin-starred and highly regarded Casa Grugno, Principe Cerami, Casa Niclodi, Ristorante Al Duomo, Granduca, Le Naumachie, La Botte and La Giara in Taormina; Ristorantino Ligny, Taverna Paradiso and Archo di Serisso in Trapani; La Nicchia in Scauri and the La Risacca in Pantelleria town.

Restaurants which are more reasonably priced between €20-€40 or around $27-$54 are Pizzeria Dietro le Mura in Aci Castello; Acquadelferro, Oste Scuro, Sotto il Convento and Il Tocco in Acireale; Il Covo Marino and L'Aragosta in Aci Trezza; A Castellana in Caccamo; La Piazzetta in Caltagirone; Portici Antico and Lido delle Palmer in Campofelice di Rocella; La Tartaruga in Capo d'Orlando; Antica Filanda in Capri Leone; Trattoria da Nino Mannino, A Pizza Sutta L'acchi, Sicilia in Bocca, Mm!!, Osteria Antica Marina, Pititto and I Cutilisci in Catania; Ristorante New Salvinius in Castellammare del Golfo; La Porta Del Re in Castiglione di Sicilia; Chat Noir, La Brace, L'Antica Corte, La Botte and Al

Travel Guide Box Set #20: The Best of Spain for Tourists + The Best of Beautiful Greece for Tourists + The Best of Italy for Tourists + The Best of Beautiful Germany for Tourists + The Best of Beautiful France for Tourists

Gabbiano in Cefalu; Drinzi in Cosellano; Mezzaparola and Al Molo in Donnalucata; Ariston in Enna; Monte San Guiliano, L'Osteria Di Venere and La Pentolaccia in Erice; Victor in Letojanni, Le Scaire in Linguaglossa, Trattoria Da Carmelo and Lido Azzuro Ristorante da Serafino in Marina di Ragusa; Trattoria Garibaldi and Mammacaura in Marsala; La Cialoma in Marzamemi; Osteria dei Sapori Perduti and La Locanda del Colonnello in Modica; Tavernna del Pavone in Monreale; Antico Orto Dei Limoni in Nicolosi; Anche Gli Angeli, Trattoria Al Crocifisso da Baglieri, Marpessa, Trattoria Fontana d'Ercole and Trattoria Il Cantuccio in Noto; Mi Manda Picone, Antica Foccaceria San Francesco, Trattoria Altri Tempi and La Cambusa in Palermo; Trattoria da Salvatore in Petralia Soprana; Azienda Agrituristica Bannata and Agriturismo Savoca which offers horseback-riding facilities as well in Piazza Armerina; Franco u' Piscaturi in Porticello; Sea Sound and Lo stadio in Pozallo; Trattoria La Bettola in Ragusa; seafood restaurants Smile, Zia Peppina and Da Carletto in Sant'Agata di Militello; Case Perrotta in Sant'Alfio; La Grotta in Santa Maria La Scala; La Gorgonia for pizza lovers and La Vignitta in Santa Tecla; Da Alfredo, Gna Sara and Moroccan-inspired Thaam in San Vito Lo Capo; Trattoria La Vecchia Conza and Porto San Paolo in Sciacca; Baqqala in Scicli; Ristorante Pizzeria Il Baglio in Scopello; La Pineta in Selinute; La Finanziera, Osteria Apollonion, La Volpe e L'Uva, Antica Locanda da Enrico, Piano B, Red Moon and contrary to its threatening English mercenary connotation Le Vin de l'Assassin Bistrot known for fish carpaccio and desserts in Siracusa; Licchios, L'incontro, Rosso DiVino, Villa Zuccaro, Arco dei Cappuccini in Taormina; La Bettolaccia, Cantina Siciliana, P&G, I Grilli Bracceria and the well-respected Tavernetta Ai Lumi in Trapani; Trattoria Mario in Ustica and the La Vela in Scauri.

For the budget conscious, cheap yet delicious meals may be availed of below €20 or an equivalent of less than $27 at Fud in Catania; Trattoria Nasca 1 in Cerda; the Niny Bar for kids specializing in ice cream in Letojanni; Antica Dolceria Bonajuto for delicious pastries and cakes in Modica; cafes Da Renato and L'Antico Chioso and Bar Alba in Mondello; Antica Caffe Spinnato and Di Martinos Special Sandwich in Palermo; La Tavernetta in Piazza Armerina; U Bagghiu in Polizzi Generosa; La Rotonda in Porticello; Pura Follia specializing in a variety of pizzas in Scicli; Fiordilatte and La Vineria Café in Siracusa; the best granita Bam Bar in Taormina; and the widely patronized Pizzeria Da Calvino in Trapani.

As an alternative to expensive restaurants, Sicily has excellent street food which can be bought from street stalls, markets or friggitorie which are stalls selling fried food. Among the street food that Sicily can be proud of are sfinciuni, which is a simple but spicy pizza with anchovies and caciovallo cheese; arancini, deep-fried rice balls with meat or vegetable fillings; pane e panelle, chick pea fritters in a hot sesame bun and some typical seafood snacks liked fried calamari, sardines and oysters.

In terms of dessert, Sicily is known for their cannoli or crunchy pastries filled with rich ricotta, chocolate and some candied fruit; cassata or sponge cake with almond paste, ricotta and sweetened fruit; gelati or ice cream, granita or sorbet and frutta alla matorana, which are marzipan-filled sweets designed as fruits.

Shopping

Shopping in Sicily is best done outdoors in its wide array of markets where beautiful handicrafts including antiques can be purchased at lower prices than in shops. In fact, it has two renowned flea markets—one in Masculucia which is held in the Piazza Trinita every second week of the month and one in Giardini Naxos, which is held on the 3rd Saturday and last Sunday of the month. From its wines and cheese made from sheep's milk aside from those produced by cows, to its desserts like the cannoli, Sicily has been known for having some of the best products in the world.

Many tourists are drawn to the shops found in the city of Agrigento, where one can find more products like high quality fashion accessories, jewelry, clothing, bags and shoes as well as food products like liquor and olive oil. For cakes and delicious desserts, Russo and Caffe Sicilia are highly recommended.

For simultaneous shopping and sight-seeing, Corso Italia and Via Roma in Ragusa would be an excellent choice as it is considered a World Heritage site by UNESCO and offers a variety of open air food markets as well.

On the otherhand, high-end shopping is often done in its capital, Palermo, which offers a lot of designer merchandise. The Corso Vittorio Emanuele would be the best choice for fashion items while L'Isola Saporito boasts of a wide array of food products.

Nevertheless, shopping centers like Le Massarie on Via A Grandi or Centro Commerciale Ibleo on Viale delle Americhe also offer the convenience of indoor shopping for those who prefer it. Other shopping centers are Etnapolis, the largest shopping center in Southern Italy with more than a hundred shops including restaurants and cinemas which is located in Catania; Catania Mall, which offers luxury designer items at affordable prices; Misterbianco Galleria Auchan, which is a large food hypermart offering clothes and mobile phones as well; Forum Palermo, which mostly carries international and designer brands; the Sicilia Fashion village in Enna, known as one of the first oultlet villages in the area which offers over a hundred well-known brands and stores; Porte di Catania Shopping Mall, which offers recreation and entertainment in addition to shopping pleasure for the entire family and I Portali, a major high-end shopping center with restaurants and recreational facilities like bowling centers and cinemas also located in Catania.

No single mafia in sight.

Travel Guide Box Set #20: The Best of Spain for Tourists + The Best of Beautiful Greece for Tourists + The Best of Italy for Tourists + The Best of Beautiful Germany for Tourists + The Best of Beautiful France for Tourists

Chapter 3 The Florentine Fulfillment

The Florentine Fulfillment

Originally known as Italy's political capital from 1865-1870, Florence evolved to become the cultural capital as the architectural and artistic works of Michelangelo, Donatello, Leonardo Da Vinci, Filippo Brunelleschi and other artistic geniuses flourished on its soil, transforming it into a huge outdoor museum.

Despite its fame as the cultural capital of Italy, it nevertheless boasts of other remarkable tourist spots like beaches, restaurants and shopping centers aside from its historic landmarks.

The Beaches in Tuscany

Based on the Blue Flag rating, Tuscany has 17 beaches which fall under the said category: Marina di Carrara, Pietrasanta, Forte dei Marmi, Camaiore and Viareggio in the high end area of Versilia where there are however, some strong currents; the Marina di Pisa, Tirrenia and Calambrone towards the south in Pisa which also tend to have strong tides, but are nevertheless suitable for families as they are shielded by large rock barriers from open sea; the Antignano, Castiglioncello, Vada di Rosignano Marittimo Quercianella, Cecina, Marina di Bibbona, Castagneto Carducci, San Vincenzo and Riotorto-Piombino in Livorno which are quite popular in Tuscany and are known to have calmer waters; the Follonica, Castiglione della Pescaia, Marina di Grosseto, Principina di Grosseto and Monte Argentario in the Maremma area in Grosseto which are the most popular among Italians and foreigners in Tuscany as they have long white and uncrowded sandy shores as well as some reef areas and finally, the Viareggio, which is the closest to Florence and the most expensive but most crowded as well.

Historic Sites

As the cultural capital, Florence naturally boasts of its numerous historic sites such as the Palazzo Pitti, a large palace which was formerly the residence of the ruling families in Florence in 1919 which is now open to the public as one of the largest art galleries in Florence; the Piazzale Michelangelo which is a large quadrangle with a glorious view over the entire capital; the Boboli Gardens created in the 1500s which boasts of sprawling green landscape accentuated by fountains and Roman antiquities such as sculptures and statues; the Basilica di San Lorenzo which is one of the most long-standing churches in Florence towering in its neo-classical grandeur of the Renaissance; the Palazzo Vecchio, which is considered as one of the most significant structures since 1872 as it has been used partly as the city hall and as museum housing major artworks pertinent to historic events; the Piazza della Signoria which is a town square frequented by many tourists for the famous sculptures of Michelangelo; the Uffizi Gallery, which is deemed as one of the greatest museums of today; the Ponte

Travel Guide Box Set #20: The Best of Spain for Tourists + The Best of Beautiful Greece for Tourists + The Best of Italy for Tourists + The Best of Beautiful Germany for Tourists + The Best of Beautiful France for Tourists

Vecchio, one of the oldest bridges most favored as a subject of photography for its renowned segmented arches and the Santa Maria del Fiore or the Duomo, which is considered the largest cathedral dome stonework in the world today featuring six centuries of architecture and artistic treasures.

Restaurants

While Italian food generally provides pure gastronomic delight for many, others may have different considerations when it comes to food. Thus, several categories are provided to help one decide in choosing where to eat in Florence. Some suggestions compiled by travelers for reasonably priced meals between €20-€40 or $27-$54 are Osteria Vini e Vecchi Sapori, which won the Traveller's Choice in 2012, Brown Sugar, Zeb and Trattoria da Ginone.

More expensive restaurants which offer meals above €40 or equivalent to more than $55 are Enoteca Pitti Gola e Cantina, the three-star or highest Michelin-rated Enoteca Pinchiorri where one can expect to spend around €155-225 or $210.88-$306.11, Ristorante Ora d'Aria and The Il Palagio.

To do as the Romans do may also be applied to the locals of Florence with respect to eating choices, as their suggestions include reasonably priced yet incredibly satisfying meals from L'Osteria di Giovanni, Il Santo Bevitore, Hostaria Il Desco which is complete with gluten free meal selections, the Ristorante Academia and the Trattoria Casalinga.

As for the cheapest meals which nonetheless satisfy one's taste for genuine Italian flavors below €20 or an equivalent of less than $27, the best recommendations are Casa del Vino, Trattoria da Mario, which has been serving traditional Tuscan meals for five decades, the Il Teatro del Sale which offers live entertainment as well, the Il Vinaino, Trattoria la Casalinga, Da Vinattieri, Sabatino and Nerbone.

Shopping in Florence

The new market or Mercato Nuovo in the middle of Florence boasts of various goods from silk to luxury goods as well as leather items and souvenirs while the sought-after factory outlets of Gucci and Prada are located just past the outskirts of the metropolis.

To be more specific, the best bargains can be found in specialty stores depending on the type of goods as follows: for the best bargains in general, the San Lorenzo market provides the best selection especially for food items in the Mercanto Centrale. Underwear is usually on sale at Intimissimi while hosiery can be availed of at low prices at Emilio Cavallini. Leather goods are abundant in Florence, although they are largely available at Borgo dei Greci. Antiques, on the other hand, are abundant in via Santo Spirito and in Piazza dei Ciompi while houseware bargains and kitchen appliances are best sought at Dino Bartolini near Via dei Servi and Bilance Carretti beside Piazza Indipendenza.

Travel Guide Box Set #20: The Best of Spain for Tourists + The Best of Beautiful Greece for Tourists + The Best of Italy for Tourists + The Best of Beautiful Germany for Tourists + The Best of Beautiful France for Tourists

Designer goods like Armani, Gucci and YSL are available at The Mall, which is just a small row of shops at very low prices. Similarly, Via dei Tornabuoni which is known for bargains on designer clothes also offers Versace, Ferragamo Bulgari and Pucci at low prices.

Meanwhile, bargains on Italian high-street fashion such as Diesel, Sisley, Benetton, Max & Co., Stefanel and Diesel can be located in the area of Via dei Calzaiuoli.

Finally, for one-stop shopping, the best department store would be Coin which is amply stocked with various goods from clothes to houseware items.

Tuscany sales including Florence often occur between January 6 until March 6 for their winter collection and from around July 15 to September 15 for their summer collection.

Then everything will be fine.

Travel Guide Box Set #20: The Best of Spain for Tourists + The Best of Beautiful Greece for Tourists + The Best of Italy for Tourists + The Best of Beautiful Germany for Tourists + The Best of Beautiful France for Tourists

Chapter 4 The Milan Mania

The Milan Mania

Known as the economic and fashion capital of Italy, Milan is surprisingly visited by tourists not only for its shopping centers but also for its various sites which draw attention including beaches and lakes, historic sites and restaurants.

Beaches and Lakes

Unlike other Italian cities which are found near coastlines, Milan is one of those which sit at quite a distance, thus it has no beaches to show off. Nevertheless, a 90-minute ride by car or train can take one to Arenzano, which is the closest beach town in Milan or two hours southwest to Liguria, which is known for its unparalleled beaches. Moreover, it is located near Lake Como which is only a short drive or train ride towards the north. Lake Como is known as one of the deepest lakes in Europe with extravagant residences and first-rate accommodations and restaurants surrounding it.

Historic Sites

Milan is also known for historic sites such as the Milan Cathedral, which is deemed the largest Gothic cathedral in history constructed over a period of nearly five centuries with more than a hundred towers and three thousand statues displayed on its roof; the Sforza castle which functions as a museum for artifacts and other works of art; the La Scala, which is an opera house which also serves as a museum for other collections of musical instruments and artistic works; the Gallery Vittorio Emanuele II which was constructed in 1867 and boasts of a colossal glass roof and a mosaic representing the united cities of Italy; the Santa Maria della Grazie which is a 15th-century convent church housing Leonardo Da Vinci's the Last Supper which inexplicably survived the bombing in World War II; the Basilica of Sant'Ambrogio which is deemed as one of the oldest churches built as early as 379 and replete in Roman architecture as well as carvings, mosaics and a golden altar.

Restaurants

An economic and fashion capital would be incomplete without one of the driving forces of their people which is—food. In fact, Milan has many well-known eating places which however are considered quite expensive such as the all-meat restaurant Ribot, Cracco, Il Salumaio di Montenapoleone, Trattoria Del Nuovo Macello, the Michelin-starred D'O, the football players' all-time favorite Giannino, Giacomo Bistrot, Dal Bolognese, Piazza Repubblica, the family-oriented Osteria Dei Cacciatori, The Grand Hotel, Al Peck Ristorante, Giancomo Arengario, Pisacco and Unico Restaurant.

As for good local food at affordable prices, the best eateries would be the El Brellin café, Bianca, L'Antico Ambrosiano, Bastianello, Rosso Pomodoro and Milan's most important bakery, Panzerotti Luini.

Shopping in Milan

For major shopaholics, the top store located in Piazza del Duomo is the 8-storey La Rinascente, the first department store for retail clothing in Milan with restaurants and cafes. Other stores which carry the big names in fashion are found in the Quadrilatero d'Oro. These are Via della Spiga, Via Manzoni, Via Sant'Andrea, Via Monte Napoleone. Via Monte Napoleone is an entire shopping street where the boutiques of the leading designers like Armani and Versace can be found.

Smaller stores also present pleasant shopping experiences contrary to the intimidating high-end ones such as those on corso di Porta Ticinese, corso Vercelli or corso Buenos Aires while the Piazza dei Mercanti is a marketplace for goods sold by small artisans and bakers at low prices.

Bargain hunters often hit sales during January and July as they are sanctioned by local government policies—a passion for fashion indeed.

Travel Guide Box Set #20: The Best of Spain for Tourists + The Best of Beautiful Greece for Tourists + The Best of Italy for Tourists + The Best of Beautiful Germany for Tourists + The Best of Beautiful France for Tourists

Chapter 5 The Roman Resplendence

Roman Resplendence

Internationally renowned for its historic significance, Rome attracts many tourists not only for its historic sites but also for its beaches, restaurants and shopping centers as well.

Beaches in Rome

Rome features some nearby beaches suitable for simply relaxing or overcoming the heat of summer such as Ostia, which is considered the most accessible as it is only around 40 minutes away from the center of Rome; the Santa Marinella, which is smaller though more attractive than Ostia and more crowded during weekends; Paradise Beach which is slightly more difficult to reach as it is located in Maccarese and Singita in Fregene, which is known as a favorable spot for romantic susnset moments by the beach.

Historic Sites

As gloriously depicted in movies, some of the most visited historic sites are the Colosseum, which is deemed the most famous building of the Roman empire used in accommodating more than 50,000 spectators for games involving gladiators and wild beasts; St. Peter's Basilica, which is the world's largest church bearing Michelangelo's magnificent interpretation of Christianity in its dome; the Pantheon, which is a temple built for pagan gods by Emperor Hadrian in 118 AD; the Circus Maximus, which was the largest stadium built and used for chariot racing in ancient Rome; the Vatican City which is the smallest state in the world; the various Arches of Constantine, Janus, Septimius Severus and Titus and other structures like the Basilica of Maxentius and Constantine; various Baths such as the Baths of Caracella and Diocletian; crypts and tombs such as the Capuchin crypt, Castel Sant Angelo, the catacombs of San Callisto and the Mausoleum of Augustus; structures of political significance such as the Flavian palace, the Forums of Augustus, Caesar and Trajan, Hadrian's Villa, the Ludus Magnus and the Mamertime Prison and various temples like the Temple of Antoninus and Faustina, Temple of Caesar, Castor and Pollux, Temple of Concord, Saturn, Venus and Rome.

Restaurants

Aside from viewing historic sites, one of the best experiences in Rome is dining. Some of the most widely acclaimed restaurants in Rome are the La Pergola with the highest rating of 3-Michelin stars, costing around €39 or an equivalent of only $53; Antica Pesa which is one of the most loved restaurants by jet setters like multi-awarded celebrity Robert De Niro and pop icon Madonna with dishes that cost surprisingly low as €15; Imago, with a rating of one-Michelin star which also boasts of patrons like JFK and classic beauties Audrey Hepburn and Grace

Kelly with meals starting at only €33 and Pipero al Rex, which specializes in meat dishes for as low as €22.

The more expensive restaurants ranging from €40 to €150 are Fortunato al Pantheon, Il Convivio di Troianai, L' Archeologia, Toscano, Il Tempio di Iside, All'Oro, Antico Arco, Glass Hostaria, Il Pagliaccio, La Pergola, L'Arcangelo, Massimo Ricciolo Ristorante Bistrot, Roscioli, Settembrini, Armando al Pantheon and Vino e Camino.

Some restaurants which serve reasonably priced meals between €20-€40 are Ditirambo, La Tavernaccia, Roa Sparita, Vascello, Cecilia Metella, Antica Birreria Peroni, Bar Necci dal 1924, Da Cesare al Casaletto, Da Felice, Da Francesco, Dal Cavalier Gino, Del Frate, Enoteca Corsi, Enoteca Provincia Romana, L'Asino d'Oro, La Campana, La Torricella, Margutta Ristorarte, Marzpane, Matricianella, Palatium, Trattoria Monti, La Gatta Mangiona, La Pratolina and Passaguai.

On the other hand, incredibly cheap yet hearty meals are served for as low as €8-€20 in Giggetto, which is known for its fried artichokes, Lilli, Marzapane, Fish Market, Arancia Blu, Ginger, Pizzarium, Pizzeria Remo, Que Te Pongo and the Restaurant Roof Garden which provides a great view of the Colloseum and the Roman Forum as well.

Other restaurants cherished by locals which tourists don't know about and might be worth exploring are Da Enzo, Osteria Bonelli, Farine, La Carbonara dal 1906 and Capo Boi.

Shopping

The most popular shopping areas in Rome are Via delCorso and Via Cola di Rienzo.

Outdoor flea markets are best for buying antiques, furniture and houseware, art, jewelry and clothing. The most important flea market in Rome and one of the largest in Europe is the Porta Portese. Flea markets known for selling antiques are those in Via del Babuino and Via Giulia. Another flea market which is more known for clothing and accessories is Via Sannio.

Rome is also known to have large food markets like Testaccio Covered amsrket and The Trinofale Market is among the largest food markets in the country.

For specific items the best shops in Rome are Eliodoro and Ashanti for precious gems and jewelry, Fabio Piccione for antique and costume jewelry, Saddlers Union for bags and luggages and other leather items including wallets and belts, Sole for textiles and fashion accessories, Society for linen and fabric, Fratelli Vigano for men's hats and head gear, Spazio IF for women's handcrafted accessories, Delfina Delettrez for fashion jewelry, Strategic Business Unit for fashionable menswear, Di San Giacomo Gioielli for shoes, Maurizio Grossi for marble and stone busts.

Travel Guide Box Set #20: The Best of Spain for Tourists + The Best of Beautiful Greece for Tourists + The Best of Italy for Tourists + The Best of Beautiful Germany for Tourists + The Best of Beautiful France for Tourists

While the standard of living in Rome is considered quite expensive, shopping for high fashion doesn't necessarily have to be done in Milan. Although designer shops on Via Condotti are not within the price range of the general public, there are, however, some shops that sell surpluses or secondhand designer items in Piazza Navona and Campo de'Fiori.

Like fashion boutiques in Milan, those in Rome also hold sales in January and July with discounts of up to 70%.

The prospects do seem bright.

Travel Guide Box Set #20: The Best of Spain for Tourists + The Best of Beautiful Greece for Tourists + The Best of Italy for Tourists + The Best of Beautiful Germany for Tourists + The Best of Beautiful France for Tourists

Chapter 6 The Venetian Venture

The Venetian Venture

Though known to many as the romantic part of Italy where couples can take gondola rides through small canals to enjoy the sights, Venice has also been acknowledged for its beaches, historical sites, food and shopping.

Beaches

Venice is known for its peaceful beaches such as Alberoni which is quieter, cheaper, family-friendly and only around 40 minutes away; Bibione, which is a spa resort bordered by a pine forest and is also easily accessible by car or by train; Rosalina beach which is around only 60 km away and can easily be reached by bus and Albarella beach which is a private beach deemed the most attractive by the Venice Beach Guide, all of which have available hotels and other relaxing accommodations.

Historical Sites

Venice is well-appreciated for many of its historical sites such as The Grand Canal, which sweeps through the entire city enabling a glimpse of the Rialto Bridge, the oldest and most famous bridge in Venice; the Piazza San Marco or St. Mark's Square, which is the most significant landmark in Venice; the Murano, which is known for its magnificent glass pieces and lamps; the Glass Museum in Palazzo Giustinian; Doge's Palace; the Bridge of Sighs which connects the palace of Doges with prison chambers transverse the Rio di Palazzo; St. Mark's Basilica or the Basilica di San Marco which is a 9th century cathedral with a stunning display of glass, mosaic and gold covered by five large domes; the Campanile di San Marco which is the tallest structure in the city where one can enjoy an incredible view of the entire metropolis; the Arsenale di Venezia, which played an important role in the growth of the Venetian Empire and the Palazzo Mocenigo, which is a spectacular palace built for one of the most prominent families in Venice.

Restaurants

Venetian cuisine is a bit different from traditional Italian cuisine as the use of fish and vegetables is highlighted.

High-end restaurants serving meals above €40 are the Alle Testiere, Antiche Carampane, Corte Sconta, Da Fiore, Il Ridotto, Locanda Cipriani, Osteria di Santa Marina, Osteria San Marco, Quadri, Riva Rosa, Riviera, Vecio Fritolin, Venissa, Acquastanca, Ai Mercanti, Al Gatto Nero, Anice Stellato, Da Rioba and Vini da Gigio.

Travel Guide Box Set #20: The Best of Spain for Tourists + The Best of Beautiful Greece for Tourists + The Best of Italy for Tourists + The Best of Beautiful Germany for Tourists + The Best of Beautiful France for Tourists

Restaurants which serve more reasonably priced meals between €20-€40 are Vineria All'Amarone, Alla Palanca, Al Portego, CoVino, Il Refolo, Impronta Café, La Bitta, La Bottega ai Promessi Sposi, la Cantina, La Zucca, L'Orto dei Mori, Muro Frari, Osteria Enoteca Ai Artisti, Osteria Al Merca, Ribot, Trattoria Ca d'Oro Alla Vedova, La Perla Ai Bisatei and Trattoria Storica.

Finally, cheap yet delicious meals ranging from below €10-€20 are available at Alla Basilica and Dai Tosi.

Shopping in Venice

Venetian markets offer a wide range of interesting products such as masks made of carefully crafted paper mache and the prestigious Murano glass pieces aside from food and art works.

For more detailed shopping, boutiques which offer specific products are Rnoldo & Battois for leather handbags; Chiarastella Cattana for textile with exclusive styles; Emilia for handmade lace and linen; Gianni Basso for exquisitely crafted stationery; Monica Daniele for special Venetian hats and outfits; Guiliana Longo for a wide selection of hats; Gilberto Penzo for model boats; Laberintho for creative and unique jewelry pieces; L'Isola for artistic glassware; Nardi for accessories and decorative objects; Venetia Stadium for luxury textile including velvet, satin and embroidered or printed silk; Anathema, for fashion accessories like scarves, Murano glass jewelry and bags; Arras for woven fabrics; Attombri for jewelry, lamps and home decors made of glass beads; Ca'Mana, for various masks ranging from carnival to sci-fi designs; Drogheria Mascari for special grocery items including balsamic vinegar and other specialties; Kalimala for leather goods such as shoes, belts, wallets and bags; L'O.FT for stylish eyewear; Madera for a variety of wares ranging from cutlery and houseware to jewelry and other accessories; Paropamiso for antique jewelry; Piedaterre for various types of footwear; Vittorio Costantini for miniature glasswork; VizioVirtu for chocolates and other sweets and Mercato di Rialto for fresh produce.

Interestingly, Venice has only one department store, Coin, which originated in there and carries various products as well as affordable clothing brands including Guess, Chanel and Swarovski.

Yet, the Venetian venture doesn't end here. After all, Rome—and all of Italy-- wasn't built in a day.

Travel Guide Box Set #20: The Best of Spain for Tourists + The Best of Beautiful Greece for Tourists + The Best of Italy for Tourists + The Best of Beautiful Germany for Tourists + The Best of Beautiful France for Tourists

Conclusion

Thank you again for purchasing this book!

I hope this book was able to help you to consider various suggestions in connection with planning a tour of Italy.

The next step is to create and enjoy your own adventure.

Finally, if you enjoyed this book, please take the time to share your thoughts and post a review on Amazon. We do our best to reach out to readers and provide the best value we can. Your positive review will help us achieve that. It'd be greatly appreciated!

Thank you and good luck!

Book 4:
The Best of Beautiful Germany for Tourists
BY GETAWAY GUIDES

The Ultimate Guide for Germany's Top Sites, Restaurants, Shopping, and Beaches for Tourists

Travel Guide Box Set #20: The Best of Spain for Tourists + The Best of Beautiful Greece for Tourists + The Best of Italy for Tourists + The Best of Beautiful Germany for Tourists + The Best of Beautiful France for Tourists

Copyright 2014 by Getaway Guides - All rights reserved.

In no way is it legal to reproduce, duplicate, or transmit any part of this document in either electronic means or in printed format. Recording of this publication is strictly prohibited and any storage of this document is not allowed unless with written permission from the publisher. All rights reserved.

Travel Guide Box Set #20: The Best of Spain for Tourists + The Best of Beautiful Greece for Tourists + The Best of Italy for Tourists + The Best of Beautiful Germany for Tourists + The Best of Beautiful France for Tourists

Table Of Contents

Introduction 63

Chapter 1 - What makes Germany a Great Travel Destination? 64

Chapter 2 - Top Tourist Spots in Germany 65

Chapter 3 - Best Beaches in Germany 71

Chapter 4 - Best Restaurants in Germany 73

Chapter 5 - Best Shopping Destinations 75

Conclusion 77

Travel Guide Box Set #20: The Best of Spain for Tourists + The Best of Beautiful Greece for Tourists + The Best of Italy for Tourists + The Best of Beautiful Germany for Tourists + The Best of Beautiful France for Tourists

Introduction

I want to thank you and congratulate you for purchasing the book, *"The Best of Beautiful Germany for Tourists: The Ultimate Guide for Germany's Top Sites, Restaurants, Shopping, and Beaches for Tourists"*.

This book contains information about Germany's beautiful tourist spots, food districts, shopping venues, and breathtaking beaches that tourist could enjoy.

If you are interested in traveling to Germany and explore its beauty and wonders, then this book is for you. This book has everything you need to know about the top tourist spots, the finest restaurants, and top shopping destinations in Germany.

Thanks again for purchasing this book, I hope you enjoy it!

Travel Guide Box Set #20: The Best of Spain for Tourists + The Best of Beautiful Greece for Tourists + The Best of Italy for Tourists + The Best of Beautiful Germany for Tourists + The Best of Beautiful France for Tourists

Chapter 1 - What Makes Germany a Great Travel Destination?

The beautiful country of Germany is situated right at the heart of Europe. Germany is one of the best travel destinations in Europe as it has many unique and fantastic sites to offer and has many wonderful tourist spots. Many visitors and tourists all over the world travel to Germany to witness the magnificence of its architectural treasures and captivating destinations that have natural beauty and splendor.

More and more people are interested in spending their much needed break from work and daily life in Germany. In fact, there has been an increase in the number of tourists who visit Germany each year. According to World Bank, around 24 million tourists visited Germany in 2009, 26 million tourists in 2010, 28million tourists in 2011, and more than 30 million tourists explored Germany in 2012. In fact, according to German National Tourism Board, Germany has been the second most popular tourist destination in Europe, next to Spain.

One of the reasons why Germany is one of the most favorite tourist destinations is the positive value-for-money ratio and different experiences and locations that the beautiful and historical country has to offer.

Surveys also show that tourists prefer Germany over other European countries because of its culture, cleanliness, security, amazing and exciting night life, modernity, and the beauty of its cities.

Germany is filled with landscapes and cities that are frequently visited for recreation and even education. Beginning in the late 18th century cities like Berlin, Munich, Dresden, and Weimar are the most popular stops of a European Grand Tour.

After the tragic Second World War has ended, Germany has instantly become a popular tourist destination for those who want to experience the richness of European history. Germany is filled with seaside resorts and spas, architectural jewels, and beautiful cities that managed to preserve their historical value and appearance. The German countryside has a pastoral aura. The cities have modern and classical feel that will make the visitors and tourists feel nostalgic and at home.

Germany is simply one of the most beautiful countries in the world.

Travel Guide Box Set #20: The Best of Spain for Tourists + The Best of Beautiful Greece for Tourists + The Best of Italy for Tourists + The Best of Beautiful Germany for Tourists + The Best of Beautiful France for Tourists

Chapter 2 - Top Tourist Spots in Germany

There are hundreds of tourist spots in Germany. In fact, there are more than ten thousand things to do when you are traveling and exploring Germany. To make sure that you get the best out of your trip to one of the most beautiful and historical places in the world, all the top tourist spots that should be included in your itinerary are all listed in this chapter.

Neuschwanstein Castle

The Neuschwanstein Castle is one of the most popular tourist spots in Germany. In fact, this magnificent and majestic castle is often listed as the top tourist spot in Germany. It has an amazing romantic architecture that will never fail to wow and amaze the tourists and visitors.

The Neuschwastein Castle is a 19th century Romanesque revival castle that peacefully sits on a beautiful rugged hill just above the village of Hohenschwangau in Bavaria, Germany. This beautiful castle was built to pay homage to Richard Wagner by Ludwig II of Bavaria. Ludwig II paid for the construction of the castle out of his personal funds and fortune.

The castle was originally built as a personal refuge and a home for the reclusive king. However, the castle was immediately opened to the paying public after the King's death in 1886. Since Ludwig's death, over sixty one million local and international tourists have visited this wonderful and elaborate palace. Over 1.3 million people visit the Neuschwanstein castle every year.

The castle has been a popular film location and many movies were filmed in the Neuschwastein Castle. Chitty Chitty Bang Bang, Space Balls, and the Wonderful World of Brothers Grimm are among the many movies filmed in this elegant and elaborate castle. This castle was also the inspiration for the Sleeping Beauty Castle of Disney. The castle has also been a finalist in the 7 Wonders of the Worlds list.

Guided castle tours are available and the castle is open daily from 8 am to 5 pm during the summer season and 9 am to 3 pm during the winter season. The castle is closed on Christmas Eve, Christmas day, New Year's Day, and New Year's Eve. Tours are facilitated by the friendly castle staff and you cannot take pictures inside the castle.

You would not only enjoy the captivating beauty of the castle, but you will also enjoy the trip to the castle. Once you get to Hohenschwangau, you have many options to get to the castle. You can also walk to the castle. This will usually take thirty to fifty minutes. You can ride a bus or you can ride in a horse-drawn carriage!

Cologne Cathedral

The Cologne Cathedral is a magnificent gothic cathedral that is known to be the hallmark and the center of the city of Cologne in Germany. It is also one of the famous landmarks in Germany and it is also one of the most visited tourist spots in the country. It is also the second tallest structure in the city of Cologne and can accommodate up to twenty thousand people. UNESCO has declared and considered the Cologne Cathedral as a World Heritage site in the year 1996 because of its impressive architecture, beautiful stained glass windows, and other works of art in this beautiful building. Tourists can also climb 509 steps of the magnificent spiral staircase to witness the scenic and beautiful view over the Rhine.

The Cologne Cathedral was built on August 15, 1248 during the Feast of the Assumption. The cathedral was built to be the refuge of the relics of the three wise men. Because of the biblical magi, the Cologne Cathedral became of the major important pilgrimage location in Germany and even in Europe.

Aside from the Shrine of the Three Wise Men which was built by Philip von Heisenberg, this splendid cathedral contains many valuable treasures. Among its treasures is a wooden sculpture called Milan Madonna or Mailänder Madonna which was made in 1290. The cathedral altar also houses the sacred relics of St. Irmgardis. The oldest large crucifix in the world called the Crucifix of Bishop Gero can also be found in this beautiful cathedral. One of the most beautiful historical pieces in the cathedral is the Five Windows located in the South side. The windows were given by Ludwig I. You can also find ancient Jewish tablets inside the cathedral.

Brandenburg Gate

The Brandenburg gate is one of the most famous landmarks in Germany. It is previously a city gate and it is located in Berlin. The serves as an entrance to the boulevard of linden trees called Unter den Linden which used to lead to the palace of former Prussian monarchs.

This magnificent historical piece was commissioned by a Prussian king, Frederick William II, as a symbol of peace. This gate was built by renowned Prussian architect Carl Gotthard Langhans in 1788. The gate was initially named Friedenstor or the Peace Gate. The sculpture on top of the gate features the image of the Goddess of Peace, Eirene.

When the Nazis rose to power, the gate became a party symbol. The gate was also partially damaged during the Second World War and when the Berlin wall fell in 1989, the Brandenburg gate became a symbol of unity and freedom.

The Brandenburg gate was restored in 2000 and it is now one of the most popular tourist and historical spots in the world. The gate is simply a breathtaking sight, especially at night. When Germany won the World Cup in 2014, the victory rally of the Germany national football team was held in front of this iconic gate.

Museum Island

The Museum Island is located in the Mitte district of Berlin in Germany. The Museum Island houses five of the most famous museums in the world. The museums occupy the northern half of this beautiful island. The Museum Island was considered as a World Heritage site by UNESCO in 1999. Here are the five museums that can be found in this amazing island.

1. The Neues Museum- This was built by Friedrich August Stüler in 1859.
2. Altes Museum – This was commissioned by Karl Friedrich Schinkel in 1830.
3. Bode Museum - This museum can be found on the northern tip of the island. This museum was opened in 1904 and was previously known as *Kaiser-Friedrich-Museum*. This beautiful museum exhibits many precious sculpture collections and many Byzantine and Antique artworks.
4. Alte Nationalgalerie – This museum was completed in 1876 and it was also designed by Friedrich August Stüler. This museum contains precious artworks donated by Joachim H. W. Wagener, a wealthy banker.
5. Pergamon Museum – This museum was considered to be the final museum of the island and was constructed in 1930. This museum contains many reconstructed historical buildings like the Ishtar Gate of Babylon and Pergamon Altar.

Dresden Frauenkirche

The Dresden Frauenkirche is a Lutheran church that is located in Neumarkt in Dresden, Germany. The original church located on the site was Roman Catholic. However, the current Baroque architectural wonder was built by Protestants. It has one of the largest and the most beautiful domes in Europe.

The church was originally built in the 18th century, however, it was destroyed during the World War II when Dresden was bombed. The church was rebuilt in 1989 and the reconstruction was completed in 2005. Although it is called a cathedral, the Frauenkirche is not the seat of the bishop.

Today, the cathedral is one of the most popular tourist spots in Germany. It also became a landmark of peace and hope in Germany.

Holstentor

The Holstentor or the Holsten Gate is one of the most beautiful city gates. It marks the western boundary of the city of Lübeck. This city gate has an impressive and magnificent brick gothic construction. It is also one relics of medieval Lübeck. Since 1987, the Holstentor has been considered as one of the certified UNESCO World Heritage sites.

The Holstentor was popular because of its imposing structure and beautiful gothic architecture. It also has the most beautiful sculptures. Today, the Holsentor serves as a museum which contains the historical relics of Lübeck including pictures and models of the old ships. The Holstentor was modernized in the year 2002 and all of the rooms inside it were redesigned. The old torture chamber was also removed.

The Holstentor is an amazing gothic historical structure that is worth visiting.

Heidelberg

The Heidelberg is a town located in the Neckar River valley and it is considered as one of the popular tourist destinations in Germany. It is also considered as one of the most beautiful places in Germany because of its picturesque and romantic cityscape. It also has many beautiful and historical structures that are simply amazing.

Here are some of the popular spots in Heidelberg that tourists must visit:

1. The Heidelberg Castle and the Old Bridge – This beautiful castle has a combination of gothic and Renaissance architectural style. It was first commissioned by Prince Elector Ruprecht III. The interior of this beautiful castle is mostly gothic, however the king's hall was built only in 1934. This hall was mainly used for events, performances, and dinner banquets. The castle is surrounded by a beautiful park where a famous poet named Johann von Goethe used to take long walks. The castle is connected to the beautiful old bridge. The bridge is a wonderful romantic structure that looks best when illuminated at night.
2. The Philosopher's walk – This strip allows you to enjoy the scenic and breathtaking view of the old town, the castle, and the old bridge. This was called the Philosopher's walk because the famous philosophers and intellectuals of Heidelberg used to walk in this pathway.
3. Churches- Heidelberg is the home of many beautiful churches like the Church of the Holy Spirit, St. Peter's Church, and The Church of the Jesuits.

Heidelberg is also a popular academic site. Tourists could visit the Heidelberg University, which is also considered as an architectural treasure. Amongst the popular structure that could be found in the university is the Studentenkarzer or the Student prison.

The Berlin Wall

The Berlin wall is a historical piece that tourists must see when they visit Germany. It has been the symbol of the cold war for twenty eight years. The wall was constructed in 1961 when the East German military men placed barbed wires to separate the East and West Berlin. It was also called as the Anti Fascist Barrier. It is 155 kilometers long and used to be riddled with trenches, attack dogs, and electric fences. At least 136 people died while trying to cross borders.

Today, the Berlin wall is a popular tourist sighting in Berlin. The wall is not filled with beautiful graffiti and what has been the symbol of division has now become a symbol of unity. Tourists can take bike tours to explore the strip.

Euro-Park

The Euro-Park is the largest and most popular theme park in Germany. It is also the second most famous theme park in entire Europe, next to Disneyland Paris. It is located in Rust, Germany. The park can accommodate up to fifty thousand guests daily and it has about four million visitors every year.

The park has twelve roller coasters and it hosts many events during the summer. The park is open from 9 am to 6 pm daily during the summer season. It is open from 11 am to 7 pm during the winter season.

The Europark is filled with rides and beautiful view. It is something that both adults and children can enjoy. The Euro-Park has about 57 rides and it is home to five resort hotels.

Tourists must not leave Germany without visiting this amazing theme park.

Romantic Rhine

The Upper Middle Rhine Valley, also known as the Romantic Rhine, has been a popular tourist destination in Germany since the 19th century. It runs between the beautiful cities of Bonn and Bingen. The Romantic Rhine is also one of the UNESCO World Heritage sites and it is a popular stopover in many European tours.

The Romantic Rhine looks like it came straight out of a story book. It has a beautiful river valley, still vineyards, and beautiful castles.

Travel Guide Box Set #20: The Best of Spain for Tourists + The Best of Beautiful Greece for Tourists + The Best of Italy for Tourists + The Best of Beautiful Germany for Tourists + The Best of Beautiful France for Tourists

There are more than fifty castles located in the Romantic Rhine. Amongst the popular castles located in this beautiful valley are the Stahleck castle, which is located in Bacharach, the Burg Pfalzgrafenstein located in Kobe, Stolzenfels Castle in Koblenz, and the magnificent Burg Rheinfels located in St. Goar.

Amongst the other popular destination in the Romantic Rhine is the Werner Chapel located in Bacharach. You can also see the highest cold water geyser in the whole world, the Andernach Geyser, in the Romantic Rhine.

The Romantic Rhine is perfect for honeymoon and vacation. It is also great for trekking. Exploring this wonderful destination is an experience that you will definitely not forget.

Oktoberfest

The Oktoberfest is an event, but many tourists around the world travel to Germany just to join the festivity. The Oktoberfest is considered to be one of the largest festivities in the world. It is held every year in Munich, Bavaria in Germany. The festival runs for 16 days from late September to the 1st weekend of October. It is one of the most important fragment of the Bavarian culture. The festival started in 1810 when Ludwig I married Princess Therese. Traditional visitors and tourists will wear Bavarian hats.

There are many attractions and events during Oktoberfest. The city is filled with beer tents, there are also a number of carnivals set up for the festivities. You would also be amazed by the opening parade and you could enjoy a wide variety of traditional German food and drinks.

In the 20th century, the festival usually opens with 12 gun salute and the tapping of the first beer keg.

Travel Guide Box Set #20: The Best of Spain for Tourists + The Best of Beautiful Greece for Tourists + The Best of Italy for Tourists + The Best of Beautiful Germany for Tourists + The Best of Beautiful France for Tourists

Chapter 3 - Best Beaches in Germany

Even if Germany is more known for its architectural structures, Germany also has the most beautiful beaches and it is known to have some of the best and most breathtaking stretches of sand in the whole Europe. If you want to just sit, relax, and enjoy the beach, here are some of the best beach destinations in Germany. Germany is also known for its nudist beaches, something that you could not find in most parts of the world.

Sylt

Sylt is a beautiful island located in Nordfriesland, Schleswig-Holstein in Germany. It is known for the unique shape of its shoreline. The beaches in Sylt are perfect if you want a peaceful and quiet time with your loved ones. The beaches in Sylt also have fine sand.

The beachfront of the wonderful island of Sylt stretches for about twenty five miles from south to north. The beaches in Sylt are wonderful for family holidays or sightseeing. You could also enjoy the clear water and powerful waves.

It is best to visit Sylt during the summer. Access to the beautiful beaches of Sylt is generally not free, the prices also vary depending on the beach that you are going to visit. Sylt also has a number of nude beaches and public beach saunas. In fact, the first nude beach in Germany was established and founded in Sylt in 1920.

Usedom

Usedom is a beautiful Baltic sea island located in Pomerania, which was divided between Poland and Germany since 1945. Usedom is known as the second largest island in Pomerania next to Rügen. It is also one of the major holiday destinations in Germany because of its beautiful beaches and natural beauty. The Island Is also known for its fine sugar white sand. This beautiful island is also accessible. You would only need to travel for about two hours and a half from Berlin to see the breathtaking beauty of this island. The beaches in Usedom are also more affordable than those in Sylt.

Rügen

Rügen is one of the most popular tourist destinations in Germany because of its beautiful beaches and amazing and majestic tall cliffs. It is the largest island in Germany. This beautiful island is located in the Pomeranian coast in the amazing Baltic sea.

There are many sightings and beaches in Rugen island, but the most popular spot and landmark in the island is the majestic cliff called the King's chair. The island is home to different luxury beach resorts tat tourists could enjoy. Tourists and visitors often can't get enough of this nostalgic and beautiful island.

St. Peter-Ording

This is a popular seaside spa town. Its seas and beaches are known for their healing powers. St. Peter-Ording's shoreline is 12 kilometers long. Walking on the beautiful beach of St. Peter- Ording is good for your mind and body.

Juist

The island of Juist is one of the only seven inhabited East Frisian Islands. It is located in Aurich in Lower Saxony, Germany. It is also called the "magic land". Juist has a beautiful 17 kilometer long shoreline. Juist is a perfect destination if you just want to enjoy the beach and has a quiet time where you can enjoy the breeze, away from the busy city life. It is also a great destination for a family vacation as kids re most likely going to enjoy the sea and the beach.

Juist is frequently visited by tourists from all over the world. In fact, tourism is the major economic source of the island.

Hiddensee

Hiddensee is a beautiful car-free Baltic island that is located west of Rugen. It is known as the "Sweet Little Isle in the Baltic Sea". The island has breathtaking beaches and it is a perfect destination for those who want a quiet time and who wants to just sit by the beach and meditate. There are also a number of hotels and hostels that are easily available to visitors and tourists.

Travel Guide Box Set #20: The Best of Spain for Tourists + The Best of Beautiful Greece for Tourists + The Best of Italy for Tourists + The Best of Beautiful Germany for Tourists + The Best of Beautiful France for Tourists

Chapter 4 - Best Restaurants in Germany

Delicious traditional German cuisine is usually one of the reasons why tourists and visitors flock to Germany. Germany is rich in tasty, satisfying food and it is also a hub of many luxurious and best restaurants that are guaranteed to give tourists an awesome dining and unforgettable dining experience. Aside from the delicious German cuisine, German restaurants also allow you to enjoy a variety of dishes from all over the world.

Spinder & Klatt

Spinder & Klatt is one of the best and popular restaurants in Germany. It is located in Köpenickerstraße, Berlin. It is a sumptuous and lavish riverside Asian Fusion club and restaurant that has a cool and relaxing ambience that tourists could enjoy.

This restaurant has a hip, sleek, and minimalist interior. It is also one of the hippest party places where young professionals and the most fashionable people in Berlin hang out and eat. The benches are Japanese-inspired while the cushioned seats and mattresses located in the dining area provide unparalleled comfort for guests. Spinder & Klatt also have an in house DJ that plays hip music while you enjoy your food. You can also lounge in a soft and comfortable sofa outside the restaurant and enjoy the beautiful view of the river.

This restaurant serves one of the best Asian fusion foods in Berlin and in Germany. The restaurant serves the delicious fillet lamb with cardamom, pumpkin and pimento puree, salmon steak, wok vegetables, and many more. They also serve the best wines. Spinder & Klatt will definitely give you a unique fine dining experience. The restaurant is open from Tuesday to Saturday 8 pm until late night.

Marktwirt

Marktwirt is one of the best restaurants in Germany and it serves the best traditional German cuisine. It is located in Heiliggeiststr, Munich and it is located right next to a popular landmark, "Viktualienmarkt" square.

Marktwirt serves the typical Bavarian cuisine and it exudes a comfortable and relaxing ambience that will enhance your overall dining experience. Restaurant employees wear traditional German clothing, which is an added attraction to tourists. You could also enjoy the beautiful garden at the back of the restaurant.

The restaurant's menu is also very inventive and it gives a little twist to the best traditional German dishes. The restaurant serves the delicious duck mousse placed in a black bread crust and roast suckling pig.

Marktwirt is definitely a place to go if you want to enjoy the best local foods Munich and Germany has to offer. It is best to book a reservation before visiting. This will ensure that you will get the best seats.

Gunnewig Rheinturm Restaurant

The Gunnewig Rheinturm is a fantastic rotating restaurant that is located in Dusseldorf, Germany. The restaurant is located at a top of a 172 meter tower and softly rotates to allow you to enjoy the beautiful view and sightings in Dusseldorf.

Dining in the Gunnewig Rheinturm restaurant will surely give you a one of a kind gastronomic experience. This amazing restaurant serves high quality international cuisine. You can enjoy different foods such as lemongrass skewer, fried perch fillet, rump steak, salads, and many more.

The restaurant can also be a good venue for events and parties. This will definitely give you the best dining experience.

East Restaurant

The East Restaurant is located I Simon-von-Utrecht-Strasse in Hamburg, Germany. East is an elegant and a stylish dining haven that has a funky lounge bar. It is one of the most popular nightlife destination in Hamburg. The restaurant has an impressive interior design and it showcases an innovative fusion of European and Asian cuisine. The restaurant serves, grilled Australian lobster with lime and asparagus that will simply give you a one of a kind culinary experience. The restaurant also has a sushi bar that guests could enjoy. The restaurant also has a wide variety of wines and champagne.

The restaurant opens and closes at different times daily, so it is best to call and reserve before visiting.

Restaurant Francais

This restaurant is definitely one of the best restaurants in Germany. It is a Michelin Star winning restaurant and it is located in the luxurious and most prominent 5 star hotel in Frankfurt, Steigenberger Frankfurt hotel.

If you want to experience a one of a kind fine dining experience then you should try Restaurant Francais. It has a relaxing and elegant ambience that will enable you to enjoy the food more. It also serves the finest and most luxurious foods such as caviar, hand dived scallops, bacon foam, Perigord truffle, and oysters.

The restaurant is open from Monday to Friday for lunch and dinner.

Travel Guide Box Set #20: The Best of Spain for Tourists + The Best of Beautiful Greece for Tourists + The Best of Italy for Tourists + The Best of Beautiful Germany for Tourists + The Best of Beautiful France for Tourists

Chapter 5 - Best Shopping Destinations in Germany

Germany is not only known for the impressive buildings, amazing tourist spots, beautiful beaches, and splendid restaurants. It is also a hub of many amazing shopping districts. It is a known fact that Germans just love to shop and shopping was even dubbed as a national pastime. While most people are used to going to malls for shopping, Germans typically shop on amazing shopping districts. Here are some of the popular shopping destinations in Germany.

Friedrichstraße

The Friedrichstraße is a major shopping and culture German street located at the heart of Berlin. This shopping street runs from Mitte to the Hallesches Tor. The street was bisected by the Berlin Wall during the Cold War and the popular Checkpoint Charlie was located in the street.

You will be fascinated with the buildings which combines the architecture of the roaring twenties and Modern Berlin.

You could visit the luxurious Quartier 206 in this street that sells designer brands, accessories, jewelries, and cosmetics. You could also find the hip shopping store Galerie Lafayette on this street.

KaDeWe or Kaufhaus des Westens

KaDeWe is one of the popular trademark department stores and shopping paradise in Germany. It is located in Wittenberg Platz, Berlin and it has around 40,000 shoppers daily. It was claimed to be the largest department store in Europe.

KaDeWe was built in 1907 and it is owned by Jewish businessman Adolf Jandorf. It has survived several wars and several highs and lows in the historical city of Berlin.

You could find just about anything in KaDeWe. It is also known as one of the most expensive shopping centers in Europe. If you want to experience the high life, it is definitely a good idea to shop at KaDeWe.

Kurfürstendamm

Kurfürstendamm is located in Berlin and it is a retail haven for the young and hip shoppers. You can find international label stores such as Zara, Benetton, and H&M in this area. You could also find designer brands such as Yves Saint Laurent in this area.

Neue Kräme

Travel Guide Box Set #20: The Best of Spain for Tourists + The Best of Beautiful Greece for Tourists + The Best of Italy for Tourists + The Best of Beautiful Germany for Tourists + The Best of Beautiful France for Tourists

Neue Kräme is one of the popular shopping districts located in Frankfurt am Main, Germany. Neue Kräme stretches up to one of the most beautiful squares in Frankfurt, Romerberg. You could see a number of antique stores and distinct designer boutiques. You could also find a number of stores for skaters and outdoor enthusiasts.

The Munich Pedestrian Zone

The Munich Pedestrian Zone is stretched from Karlsplatz to Marienplatz. This shopping street is usually packed. You can find huge and popular department stores in the area such as Karstadt and Galleria Kaufhof. You can also find international fashion stores like H&M, Hirmer, and Zara in the area.

Königsallee

Königsallee is a major shopping street in Düsseldorf. This shopping street is the hub of many high end designer shops, the most elegant and luxurious boutiques, and the most exquisite shopping malls in Germany.

Mönckebergstraße

Mönckebergstraße is a popular shopping street in Hamburg, Germany. This street is the hub of Karstadt, the largest sports store in Europe, and Saturn, the largest electronic store in the World. You could also find many popular department stores in the area.

Travel Guide Box Set #20: The Best of Spain for Tourists + The Best of Beautiful Greece for Tourists + The Best of Italy for Tourists + The Best of Beautiful Germany for Tourists + The Best of Beautiful France for Tourists

Conclusion

Thank you again for purchasing this book!

I hope this book was able to help you to find the best tourist spots, restaurants, beaches, and shopping streets in Germany.

The next step is to explore and see the beauty of Germany. Use this book to guide you in exploring and experiencing the wonders of Germany. Discovering the its splendor and magnificence is one of the most pleasant and unforgettable experience that you will ever have in your life.

Finally, if you enjoyed this book, please take the time to share your thoughts and post a review on Amazon. We do our best to reach out to readers and provide the best value we can. Your positive review will help us achieve that. It'd be greatly appreciated!

Thank you and good luck!

Book 5:
The Best of Beautiful France for Tourists
BY GETAWAY GUIDES

The Ultimate Guide for France's Sites, Restaurants, Shopping and Beaches for Tourists

Travel Guide Box Set #20: The Best of Spain for Tourists + The Best of Beautiful Greece for Tourists + The Best of Italy for Tourists + The Best of Beautiful Germany for Tourists + The Best of Beautiful France for Tourists

Copyright 2014 by Getaway Guides - All rights reserved.

In no way is it legal to reproduce, duplicate, or transmit any part of this document in either electronic means or in printed format. Recording of this publication is strictly prohibited and any storage of this document is not allowed unless with written permission from the publisher. All rights reserved.

Travel Guide Box Set #20: The Best of Spain for Tourists + The Best of Beautiful Greece for Tourists + The Best of Italy for Tourists + The Best of Beautiful Germany for Tourists + The Best of Beautiful France for Tourists

Table Of Contents

Introduction 81

Chapter 1 What to Know About France 82

Chapter 2 Sites to Visit 83

Chapter 3 Food and Dinning 86

Chapter 4 Shopping in France 91

Chapter 5 Beach Guide 94

Conclusion 96

Check Out My Other Books 97

Travel Guide Box Set #20: The Best of Spain for Tourists + The Best of Beautiful Greece for Tourists + The Best of Italy for Tourists + The Best of Beautiful Germany for Tourists + The Best of Beautiful France for Tourists

Introduction

I want to thank you and congratulate you for purchasing the book, *"The Best of Beautiful France for Tourists"*.

This book contains proven steps and strategies on how to enjoy and take advantage of your visit to France.

People associate France with beautiful Renaissance architecture, warm delicacies like the croissant and their distinct fashion style. France is listed as the most popular tourist destination in the world. It attracts about 80 million tourists every year on average. It is one of the leading cultural destinations in the world and is one of the sites where many International events are held.

Tourists also go to France to experience Parisian cuisine and a taste of Parisian fashion. The museums, cathedrals and palaces also provide a peak at France's culture, and how the country looked magnificent, even a few hundred years before. The France travel experience also provides enough variety to suit different tastes and preferences.

The romantic allure of France has not faded in time and in fact continues to attract people from people all over the world. France is one of the destinations that you should not miss. There are various attractions to see and many other untouched places to enjoy.

Thanks again for purchasing this book, I hope you enjoy it!

Travel Guide Box Set #20: The Best of Spain for Tourists + The Best of Beautiful Greece for Tourists + The Best of Italy for Tourists + The Best of Beautiful Germany for Tourists + The Best of Beautiful France for Tourists

Chapter 1 What to know about France

France is the most visited country in the world. People just love seeing the beautiful countryside along with the rich culture, food, language and customs that describe the Parisian life.

Although people have various reasons why they wanted to go to France, everyone is captivated by its rich culture and heritage. Some of the tourists also ended up living in France full time. However, just like any place in the world, France also has its own share of unique etiquette that you should know about before visiting the country.

Customs

French people are very observant and like to look at people. They often sit at cafes to look at passersby. You might catch them looking at what you are wearing or what you are reading.

It is also a French custom to great people by kissing their cheeks instead of shaking their hand. They do like to kiss both man and woman so if you are not comfortable about it, just extend your hands first to express that you would rather shake hands. Also, kissing does not mean that you have to literally smack your lips into their cheeks. French practice bisous, which is a kiss where the cheeks lightly touch. Maintain eye contact whenever you are talking to other people. This shows that you are interested in what they are saying.

French locals also do not like the noise made by excited tourists. This might cause them to raise their eyebrows or even sigh. Be sure to be aware of your surroundings and lower your voice whenever you are at churches, theaters, cinemas and museums.

One of the most known customs in France is greeting people before talking to them. A simple 'bonjour' or 'merci' are considered as words of politeness. You should also greet the staff of restaurants once you enter the shop.

When in town

The French have a distinct sense of personal space. If you are invited to their home, they will usher you to a guest area and is expected to stay there. Also, be sure to bring a gift if you are invited to dinner and maintain good manners while on the dinner table.

Language

One of the best ways to look unlike the average tourist is to learn little French. The French can appear unfriendly to English speaking tourists so it really helps if you try to speak little French.

Travel Guide Box Set #20: The Best of Spain for Tourists + The Best of Beautiful Greece for Tourists + The Best of Italy for Tourists + The Best of Beautiful Germany for Tourists + The Best of Beautiful France for Tourists

Chapter 2 Sites to visit

France is the most famous tourist destination for a reason. The country and beautiful cultural heritage attracts tourists from all over the world. Additionally, France also has a good climate and beaches where tourists can enjoy various activities from summer to winter.

Chartes Cathedral

The highly preserved Chartes Cathedral is one of the best examples of the French gothic architecture. The cathedral is located about 50 miles from Paris. Almost all the details of the architecture are original. The sculptures as well as the stained glasses are originals. The Chartes Cathedral has also been a pilgrimage destination in the Middle Ages. Its remarkable history has impressed even nonreligious visitors.

According to early records, the Chartes Cathedral has been used to house the tunic of the Virgin Mary known as the Sancta Camisia. The holy relic was said to have been given by Charlemagne after it was given to him as a gift during a trip to Jerusalem. Remarkably, the cathedral was never looted nor destroyed during the French revolution and the restorations have never altered the architecture of the church.

The Great Dune of Pyla

The great dune of Pyla in France is the tallest sand dune in Europe. The dune almost measures about 500 meters in width and 3 km in length. During the recent years, the dune is slowly being pushed back into the forest. The rate which it moves varies considerably, sometimes it moves less than a meter but is now slowly covering the roads and constructions near it.

Palais des Papes

The Palais des Papes or the Palace of the Popes is the main attraction of Avigon. It is a vast castle that holds significant historical, religious and architectural importance in France. It is also one of the Gothic churches in Europe.

Avigon became the home of the Popes in 1309 after the clergy fled the chaos of Rome. The structure was built in the rocky edge of north Avignon. The palace was built in two phases with two segments. Once it was completed, it occupied at least 2.6 acres.

The palace was under the papal control for over 350 years where it gradually deteriorated despite efforts to repair it. It became a revolutionary site when it was taken by forces in the 16th century. The Palais de Papes is open to the public and houses public archives and artifacts.

Chateau de Chambord

Travel Guide Box Set #20: The Best of Spain for Tourists + The Best of Beautiful Greece for Tourists + The Best of Italy for Tourists + The Best of Beautiful Germany for Tourists + The Best of Beautiful France for Tourists

The chateau de Chambord is the second most popular chateau in France after Versailles and is considered as one of the masterpiece of the French Renaissance. The building was never fully completed. It was commissioned by King Francis I so that he could be near the Countess of Thoury, his mistress. It is also built to serve as a hunting lodge for the king. Some authors suggest that the chateau was heavily influenced by the French architect Philibert Delmorme while others say that Leonardo da Vinci added some of the significant details of the chateau.

The Verdon Gorge

Gorge du verdon rises from the Verdon River where it was named. Its bright green color is one of its best features. Verdon is located at the region of Provence, crossing over the Var and the Alps. The Verdon is also considered as one of the most beautiful natural attractions in Europe and are visited by hikers and campers since 1990.

The gorges date backs around 200 million years ago when one part of France was still under water. This enabled limestone and coral deposits on the gorge which can still be seen today. When the water subsided, the deposits result in distinctive rock formations around the landscape. Tourists also enjoy different water sport activities in the area like water skiing, kayaking and rafting.

Mont Saint-Michel

Mont Saint Michel is an island that is located at the coast of Normandy. The beautifully preserved Abbey of St. Michel stands at the top of a rocky island. It is surrounded by various streets and medieval architecture. The Abbey was built for monks in 708 AD after the current bishop was said to have been visited by Archangel Michael. This has also made it popular as a pilgrimage point.

The island can be reached by buss from Rennes and Pontorson since it is connected to the mainland. The tourists will also enjoy various selections of restaurants and cafes in the small village bellow.

The palace of Versailles

The palace was built by King Louis XIII and has remained as the official residence of King of France until 11789 during the French Revolution. The chateau is one of the most popular destinations in France and is usually visited by about 3 million tourists every year.

The palace boasts of many features including the Hall of Mirrors which composes of 17 mirrored arches. Tourists can also see the hidden passage used by Marie Antoinette to escape the revolution. Even the salon has painted ceilings and wonderful decorations. Visitors should not miss the 250 acre garden with its geometrical pattern of trees and pathways.

Chamonix

Chamonix is a popular resort at the bottom of Mont Blanc. It also hosted the first Winter Olympics in 1924 where skiers and boarders from all over the world were put to the test against the challenging slopes of the mountain. The site also attracts mountain climbers and extreme sports enthusiasts. Chamonix is connected to the valley by railway and highway. The town has a lot of stores that provide a collection of local shops and sporting equipment.

St Tropez

St Tropez is a provincial town located 65 miles from Marseille and is located on the French Riviera. It was used as a military foothold at the beginning of the 20th century. After the war has subsided, it became a popular resort destination.

St Tropez is known for its rich guests that come every summer. It has been dubbed as one of the favorite spots for jetsetters, millionaires and fashion models. The surrounding area of St Tropez showcases the Maures Mountains. It also has a very beautiful sea side.

Eiffel Tower

No trip to France would be complete without a visit to the Eiffel Tower. Eiffel Tower has become the symbol of Paris and the most famous attraction in France. The tower was built by Gustav Eiffel as an arch to the International Exhibition.

The Eiffel tower has three levels for visitors with the restaurants located at the first and second floors. The third level is the observatory platform which rises 276 meters above the ground. You can access the tower through the Paris Metro.

Travel Guide Box Set #20: The Best of Spain for Tourists + The Best of Beautiful Greece for Tourists + The Best of Italy for Tourists + The Best of Beautiful Germany for Tourists + The Best of Beautiful France for Tourists

Chapter 3 Food and Dinning

Your tour will not be complete without visiting French restaurants that offer delectable cuisine.

Brasseries

Brasseries are inns that make their own beer. On modern times, they are more identified with their white linen and homemade hooch. Brasseries often serve seafood and regional specialties.

Brasserie Mollard (115 rue Saint-Lazare. 8e)

The Brasserie Mollard seems to be frozen it time with its nouveau décor. Everything has been polished to look like it was still 1985. The marble columns, mosaics and ceramic frescoes to the lamps and furniture show classic art.

The food is also frozen in time. The brasseries have a seafood bar complete with fresh shellfish, lobsters, and trout and other classic dishes and dessert. The service is also very old school. The place attracts tourists, locals and even seniors.

Terminus Nord (23 Rue de Dunkerque, 75010)

The Terminus Nord is considered as the epitome of Parisian restaurant. Its grand area is decorated in deco style and Art Nouveau which gives the place a traditionally classic vibe. The brasserie welcomes foreign tourists and locals who want to experience traditional French cuisine.

Classic Bistros

Classic bistros are a hangout for many locals. It has a homey and warm atmosphere which offers earthy classic dishes and few specials.

Bistro Volnay (8 rue Volney, 2e)

The art decoration in Bistro Volnay attracts local businessmen during lunch. This bistro is located near an Opera. Meal starters are usually light in flavor followed by main dishes with powerful flavors. You will also enjoy classic desserts like crème caramel and soufflé on the menu.

Café Constant (132 rue Saint Dominique 7e)

Café Constant is popular among locals and tourists so it is almost always full. The blackboard menu shows the daily specials. There is always classic French cuisine like veal cordon bleu but it the bistro can also serve sophisticated dishes. Café Constant is also famous for its delicious desserts made from high quality ingredients.

Chez Dumonet (117 rue du Cherche- Midi, 6e)

Travel Guide Box Set #20: The Best of Spain for Tourists + The Best of Beautiful Greece for Tourists + The Best of Italy for Tourists + The Best of Beautiful Germany for Tourists + The Best of Beautiful France for Tourists

This classic bistro uses luxury ingredients and employs classic bistro cooking. It has a traditional setting with its dark walls and cast iron radiators. The bistro also allows half portions which allow you to taste a variety of dishes without spending full.

Chez Grenouille (52 rue Blanche, 9e)

This classic bistro is hidden behind the theatre district so it is easy to walk pass it. It also has unassuming decorations with its walls only decorated with awards. However, it is constantly packed with locals. The menu composes of traditional cooking of Alexs Blanchard who is known for recreating classic dishes. The specialty of the Chez Grenouille varies from sweetbread to steak. There is no a la carte meal but rather has a three course dinner menu. Make sure to leave room for dessert since the bistro offers very tempting selections.

L'Auberge du 15 (15 rue de la santé 13e)

You can expect high quality classic French cuisine in L ' Auberge at a more affordable price. The bistro cultivates a country vibe with its open kitchen and hunting motifs on walls. The food is likely compared to farmhouse kitchen servings and tableside theatre. There are also reasonably priced bottles of wines with variety of options.

La Gauloise (59 avenue de la Motte-Picquet 15e)

La Gauloise attracts various high end customers such as theater directors, politicians, prizewinning writers and tourists. It design is welcoming and very chic with an eye for discretion. The tables are well spaced apart and provides great service.

The cooking has developed in time but has never strayed from seasonal and traditional dishes. The menu is also reasonably priced which attracts not just dignitaries but youth as well.

Le Bougainville (5 rue de la Banque, 2e)

In the chic side of France, it is quite surprising to find a bistro that seems to remain unchanged since 1950s. The tables and brick red banquettes to the parquet flooring have remained untouched. They still offer classic dishes with fine slices of beef and fried. It can be complemented with the bistro's wide range of chocolate desserts.

Le Garde- Temps (19 bis rue Fontain, 9e)

The Garde-Teps provides polite and unfussy service with the dishes geared towards southwest delicacies with a touch of traditional flavors. The meal starts with classic dishes and ends with delectable desserts. Their cheeses are considered a specialty. There is no need for reservation since this place is so big that it is never packed full.

Travel Guide Box Set #20: The Best of Spain for Tourists + The Best of Beautiful Greece for Tourists + The Best of Italy for Tourists + The Best of Beautiful Germany for Tourists + The Best of Beautiful France for Tourists

Modern Bistros

Modern bistros are rooted in classic tradition but with its own contemporary flavor. Most modern bistros keep their menu fresh and update it daily or weekly.

Abri (92 rue du Faubourge Poissonniere, 10e)

Abri is a pocket sized restaurant that is right next to the metro. It is famous for its multi layered and stacked sandwiches that are put together by a foreign Japanese chef, Katsuaki Okiyama. This results in a delicious blend of French and Japanese cuisine. Since the place is not too big, you will have to be patient and have to reserve a table.

La Table d' Eugene (18 rue Eugene Sue 18e)

This bistro is named after the novelist Eugene Sue. The gourmet cuisine is affordable and boasts magnificent food bursting with simple flavors and beautifully presented.

Le Galopin (34 rue Sainte-Marthe, 10e)

This is a little restaurant set at Sainte-Marthe square. Its menu composes of creative and unique dishes that vary accordingly to the mood of the chef. The avant-garde chef of this bistro takes unfashionable vegetables and turns them into fashion cuisine. The dishes are inspired by traditional delicacies.

Le Hide (10 rue General Lanrezac, 17 e)

Le Hide is a regular spot for people who enjoy Japanese cuisine at a reasonable price. You can expect dishes like tender faux fillet steak and duck with pear and thyme sauce.

Pierre Sang Boyer (55 rue oberkampf, 11e)

The food served in Pierre Sang Boyer is popular among clients who like Asian inspired dishes. The chef is also one of the finalists in Top Chef and occasionally interrupts his cooking to pose for photographs for his customers.

Quick bites

France has its own version of fast food with their salty seafood, giant burgers and chef twist's on tapas.

Atao (86 rue Lemercier, 17e)

Atao looks like a fisherman' cabin with its blue color and wooden exterior. It even has fresh flowers and an anchor and flag from old Brittany. Candlelight enhances the mood better. One of its specialties is fine oysters from fine native varieties to Japanese cruses.

Big Fernand(55 rue du Faubourge Poissonniere, 9e)

This is a brilliant burger chain that draws its inspiration from the American favorite burger with its own French twist. The ingredients are taken from all over France. The menu has five main burgers but you can always ask to build you own.

Frenchie Bar a Vins (5 rue du Nil, 2e)

The Frenchie Bar provides an Anglo take on bistro cooking. This is the kind of place where people freely intermingled with each other.

Parisian chic dinning

Parisian restaurants provide genuine dining experience, spectacular view and beautiful interior that can only be found in France.

Akrame(19 rue Lauriston, 16 e)

Akrame is one of the hottest locations in Paris ever since it opened. There s no menu in Akrame, instead it has opted to serve dishes depending on the flavor of the day. Akrame provides a three course meal for a good value.

La tour d' Argent (15 quai de la Tournelle, 5e)

This chic restaurant is starting to regain its popularity after the death of its original owner. The owner is being creative in unique dishes like giant langoustine with coffee foam.

La Table du Lancaster (7 rue de berry, 8e)

La Table du Lancaster is safely hidden from the Hotel Lancaster. The restaurant can be described as timelessly elegant. It usually serves simple and beautifully cooked dishes.

Petrelle

Petrelle's cuisine and decoration attracts film stars and designers. The owner ensures that the dishes are made from the finest ingredients. The menu is all in a la carte and it tends to change depending on the season.

Restaurant du Palais-Royal (110 galerie Valois, 1er)

The restaurant boasts its interior and exterior set up. This place attracts dignitaries and locals. Restaurant du Palais-Royal specializes in risotto and Black, Black and Lobster.

Regional cuisine

Breizh Café (109 rue Vieille du Temple, 3e)

Breizh Café has a modern chic exterior and is quite different from the regular creperie. You might want to start off with the creuse oysters before you indulge to the main meals like the galette.

Travel Guide Box Set #20: The Best of Spain for Tourists + The Best of Beautiful Greece for Tourists + The Best of Italy for Tourists + The Best of Beautiful Germany for Tourists + The Best of Beautiful France for Tourists

L'Ambassade d' Auvergne (22 rue du Grenier Saint-Laxare, 3e)

L'Ambassade d' Auvergne is a rustic style restaurant at the central district of France. It serves a variety of dishes in large servings.

French wine is heralded as one of the best in the world. While the food is outstanding, you should also enjoy various wine selections while in France. Be sure to order and even indulge in a glass of wine to complete your dining experience.

Travel Guide Box Set #20: The Best of Spain for Tourists + The Best of Beautiful Greece for Tourists + The Best of Italy for Tourists + The Best of Beautiful Germany for Tourists + The Best of Beautiful France for Tourists

Chapter 4 Shopping in France

France is one of the leading capitals of fashion industry. Parisians enjoy window shopping and mostly purchase their clothes outdoors in coveted shopping districts like the Champ-Elysees and Marais. Here are the three top shopping destinations if you want to find a one-stop district.

Forum des Halles Shopping Center

This shopping district is right in the middle of Paris. It is designed like a giant labyrinth when it was first opened in 1970 after the demolition of the market. It also has a massive underground shopping complex where you have to ride two escalators to access it. It is quite difficult to navigate through the center but the convenience and variety make up for it. You can also find mid-range brands like Zara and H&M in the area.

Carrousel du Louvre

This shopping district is open seven days a week and is at the heart of Paris. It is just below Louvre Museum's pyramid. This is an ideal place to shop if you wish to find high quality goods, books, electronics, accessories and gifts. Many locals also visit this area for the Apple Store. There are also luxury gifts and jewelry in the area. After your shopping spree, you can enjoy gourmet food at the upper level of the shopping district. Major stores in the shopping district include Virgin Megastore, Bodum, Lalique and Esprit.

Les Quatre Temps Shopping Center at La Defense

This shopping center is in the business district of the city known as La Defense. It has impressive views of the grande Arche de la Defense. It is easily accessible by train. It is home to several mid-range stores as well as restaurants and cinemas. Major stores include Zara, Desigual, H&M, Lancel and American Apparel.

Budget shopping

Being fashionable and luxurious can be pretty easy in France, however, several people want to shop on budget districts. Parisians are known how to choose the perfect slacks from a discount store without sacrificing the quality.

Vide Greniers or Attic Sales

The best way to find affordable items is at yard sales. While you will not find it at the middle of the city, Parisians also have their own way of selling their old household items. These attic sales can also hold secondhand clothes. People who can dig for items can certainly find braded items for a fraction of the price.

Paris Vintage Stores

Parisians like classic and elegant fashion so they also support various vintage shops in Paris. There are vintage shops in every neighborhood where you will always find items for sale.

You can find vintage shops in Montmartre behind the metro Abbesses which carries a dynamic mix of funky clothes for women. The area in Hotel de ville and Centre Pompidou also has many vintage shops. Free'P'Star is a vintage shop that carries an assortment of jeans, shoes and shirts for few Euros. These shops are usually within a walking distance from each other.

You should also check Frip Sape which offers secondhand items including a good selection of leather boots. Goldy mama carries high end pieces from top designers like Channel and Jean-Paul Gaultier. The friendly staff can also help you find what you need.

Kookai Stock

Kookai Stock is located at rue Reaumur at the second district. The store offers ready to wear items for women for half the price. The items usually come from last season or surplus from the current collection.

Global chains

If you do not have time or patience to scour for second hand items, you can check out global chains like Promod, Zara and H&M for year round low price fashion. Each store has a different style so you will most likely find one that suits your preference. You find these stores at most of the major shopping district in Paris.

Flea Market

Flea markets also offer great selection of clothes and are part of the culture. You can find these markets at Clingancourt/St Ouen. It might be overwhelming at first sight but it will also be worth your while to check these markets.

Andre Stock

Shoes are notoriously expensive in Paris for its high quality. Andre offers great alternative for a fraction of the price. The styles may change constantly so you might need to visit the store regularly to find what you are looking for.

Summer and Winter Sale

Sales are actually regulated in France and are conducted twice a year: in summer before it gets really hot and in winter following Christmas. Boutique, stores and designer outlets clear out items from the previous season. You need to bargain like a Parisian to take advantage of the sale.

- Be early. The best deals in Paris can be found shortly after it has opened. Most Parisians also get ready for the sale by trying the clothes one day before and deciding what they want to buy. When the day of sale arrives, they only need to look for the item then pay for it.

- Avoid frenzy. Sales in Paris are well known so you have to be patient and have enough energy to survive it. The best time to hit the stores is during the week during the early morning or lunch hours. Parisians even take a day off from work to go to the sale.

- Dress lightly and comfortably. Dress in simple garments that can be easily taken off to save time in the fitting room. You should also wear comfortable shoes since you may need to run around to find what you are looking for.

- Balance the quality and price. You can also wait until the midpoint of the sale to shop since this is when the second mark down happens. Waiting until the end of the sale may give you several discounts but you will have fewer options then.

- Shop around and read the label. Compare prices in several stores and do not forget to read the exchange policy on each item.

Travel Guide Box Set #20: The Best of Spain for Tourists + The Best of Beautiful Greece for Tourists + The Best of Italy for Tourists + The Best of Beautiful Germany for Tourists + The Best of Beautiful France for Tourists

Chapter 5 Beach guide

France has different beaches that can suit nature lovers, families, campers and water sport enthusiasts.

Porto-Pollo

This beach is just a two hour flight from London or Manchester. It has a long stretch of white sand beach that is surrounded y green hills. Your trip will not be complete without exploring the crystal clear water filled with colorful fish.

Baie d'Audierne

Baie d'Audierne has 2,000 km coastline. Walking the sandy beach really feels like you are walking on the edge of Europe. Families can find relaxation in places like Pors Carn. You can also enjoy lively activity in Pointe de la Torche.

L'Ile de Riou, Marseille

L'Ile de Riou is a perfect beach getaway for people who enjoys diving. The wild and uninhabited beach is only accessible by boat. The beach is now the scuba starting point for many expeditions around the area.

Euronat, Cote d'Argent, Aquitaine

This beach is surrounded by pine woods and is almost untouched by mass tourism. This is a perfect place for nature lovers. You can see laid back villages where most families stay to unwind.

Plage de l'Almanarre, Provence-Alpes

This is a good spot for sports and recreational activities. The sand extends for 4 km and connects to the town of Giens. One area is even reserved for kite surfers and windsurfers.

Plage de Meneham

You can discover some of France's best white sand beaches by taking the road between Meneham and Neis Vran. You can see beautiful coves and rocky outcrops on the deserted shores. Motor homes are also welcome in the area and can park overnight for free.

Argeles Plage, Languedoc- Roussillon

The beach is located at the Mediterranean beach and is perfect for families. It has an 8 km stretch of golden sand with clear blue waters that never gets crowded. It is also beautifully maintained and also has great facilities.

Beaulieu-sur-Mer, French Riviera

This is the most recommended beach for families with little children. They can swim on shallow water until they reach the floating trampoline which they can use to jump off into the water.

Cote Sauvage, Poitou-Charentes

The beach is surrounded by tall pines and can only be accessed by a 10 minute hike. It has a 30 km of unadulterated white sand beach. This is one of the best wild beaches in France so do not expect souvenir shops and beach umbrellas.

Conclusion

Thank you again for purchasing this book!

I hope this book was able to help you to explore France better.

The next step is to visit France and experience different adventure.

Finally, if you enjoyed this book, please take the time to share your thoughts and post a review on Amazon. We do our best to reach out to readers and provide the best value we can. Your positive review will help us achieve that. It'd be greatly appreciated!

Thank you and good luck!

Travel Guide Box Set #20: The Best of Spain for Tourists + The Best of Beautiful Greece for Tourists + The Best of Italy for Tourists + The Best of Beautiful Germany for Tourists + The Best of Beautiful France for Tourists

Check Out My Other Books

Below you'll find some of my other popular books that are popular on Amazon and Kindle as well. Simply click on the links below to check them out. Alternatively, you can visit my author page on Amazon to see other work done by me.

The Best of England For Tourists

http://amzn.to/1rv7RVZ

The Best of Beautiful Greece For Tourists

http://amzn.to/1u9Xclw

The Best of Italy For Tourists

http://amzn.to/1kNIqYm

The Best of Spain For Tourists

http://amzn.to/1zHGGII

The Best of Beautiful Germany For Tourists

http://amzn.to/V4S0iT

The Best of Beautiful Netherlands For Tourists

http://amzn.to/1oU2hKF

The Best of Brazil For Tourists

http://amzn.to/1sC0SdT

Travel Guide Box Set #20: The Best of Spain for Tourists + The Best of Beautiful Greece for Tourists + The Best of Italy for Tourists + The Best of Beautiful Germany for Tourists + The Best of Beautiful France for Tourists

If the links do not work, for whatever reason, you can simply search for these titles on the Amazon website to find them.

Made in the USA
Coppell, TX
11 September 2024

37040148R10056